WILD EDIBLE PLANTS

of Western North America

DONALD R. KIRK

illustrated by
JANICE KIRK

NATUREGRAPH PUBLISHERS

Library of Congress Cataloging in Publication Data CIP

Kirk, Donald R
   Wild edible plants of the Western United States.

   Bibliography: p.
   Includes index.
   1. Plants, Edible—The West.   I. Title.
QK98.5.U6K57   1975   581.6'32'097   75-5998

COVER: "Thorn Apple" photo by Donald R. Kirk
           Design by David A. Duncan

ISBN 0-87961-037-9   Cloth edition
ISBN 0-87961-036-0   Paper edition

Published by Naturegraph Publishers, Inc., Happy Camp, Ca 9603

PLATE I

129. *Grindelia squarrosa*
Gum Plant

116. *Lomatium* sp.
Biscuitroot

88. *Prunus virginiana*
Chokecherry

148. *Taraxacum* sp.
Dandelion

PLATE II

167. *Brodiaea* sp.
Brodiaea

43. *Monolepis nuttalliana*
Patata

249. *Cowania mexicana*
Cliffrose

162. *Trillium ovatum*
Coast Trillium

PLATE III

71. *Prunella vulgaris*
Self Heal

103. *Epilobium angustifolium*
Fireweed

12. *Erodium cicutarium*
Alfilarea

69. *Agastache urticifolia*
Horsemint

PLATE IV

100. *Urtica lyallii*
Nettle

154. *Smilacina stellata*
Star-flowered Solomon Seal

272. *Acer grandidentatum*
Big-tooth Maple

258. *Cercidium microphyllum*
Palo Verde

PLATE V

256b. *Prosopis pubescens*
Screwbean

256a. *Prosopis juliflora*
Mesquite

40. *Polygonum amphibium*
Water Persicaria

261. *Dalea terminalis*
Pea Bush

PLATE VI

231. *Echinocactus* sp.
Barrel Cactus

160. *Lilium pardalinum*
Leopard Lily

65. *Castilleja* sp.
Indian Paint Brush

144. *Tragopogon* sp.
Salsify

PLATE VII

161. *Calochortus tolmiei*
Star Tulip

161. *Calochortus venustus*
White Mariposa

96. *Vicia* sp.
Vetch

35. *Montia sibirica*
Miner's Lettuce

PLATE VIII

117. *Heracleum lanatum*
Cowparsnip

161. *Calochortus nuttallii*
Sego Lily

40. *Polygonum bistortoides*
Knotweed

265. *Juglans californica*
Walnut

PLATE IX

252. *Heteromeles arbutifolia*
Toyon

155. *Streptopus amplexifolius*
Twistedstalk

154. *Smilacina racemosa*
False Solomon Seal

107. *Shepherdia canadensis*
Russet Buffaloberry

PLATE X

122. *Lonicera utahensis*
Utah Honeysuckle

87. *Rosa* sp.
Wild Rose

108. *Rhus trilobata*
Squaw Bush

122. *Lonicera involucrata*
Twinberry

PLATE XI

285. *Yucca baccata*
Soap Weed

285. *Yucca brevifolia*
Joshua Tree

134. *Artemisia* sp.
Sagebrush

59. *Asclepias speciosa*
Milkweed

PLATE XII

144. *Tragopogon dubius*
Salsify

25. *Brassica campestris*
Mustard

244. *Tecoma stans*
Trumpet Bush

126. *Helianthus* sp.
Sunflower

PLATE XIII

27. *Nasturtium officinale*
Water Cress

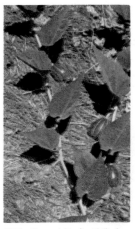

275. *Cucurbita foetidissima*
Buffalo Gourd

?1. *Symphoricarpos rivularis*
Snowberry

133. *Achillea millefolium*
Yarrow

PLATE XIV

48. *Sarcobatus vermiculatus*
Greasewood

119. *Galium aparine*
Goosegrass

44. *Atriplex hymenelytra*
Desert Holly

41. *Chenopodium fremontii*
Goosefoot

PLATE XV

271. *Aesculus californica*
Buckeye

281. *Chlorogalum pomeridianum*
Soap Plant

40. *Polygonum bistortoides*
Knotweed (rootstock)

19. *Cleome lutea*
Bee Plant

PLATE XVI

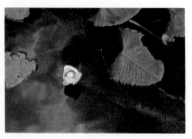

9. *Nuphar polysepalum*
Pond Lily

159. *Fritillaria lanceolata*
Fritillary

54. *Vaccinium ovatum*
Huckleberry

194. *Gaultheria shallon*
Salal

TABLE OF CONTENTS

ACKNOWLEDGMENTS

I am particularly grateful to Charles G. Davis, Professor of English at Boise State University, Boise, Idaho, for reading in its entirety the first portion of this book, and a number of the plant entries. His suggestions led to greater clarity of writing. Thanks go also to W. Douglas Patterson of the Biology Department of Shasta College, Redding, California, for providing me with nearly 50 specimens needed for the preparation of illustrations, and he also helped me in other ways.

I am also grateful to the Herbarium, University of California, Berkeley, for the loan of 270 specimens essential to the preparation of the illustrations. Dr. Robert Ornduff, of the Herbarium staff, gave me efficient help.

Other herbaria that were helpful were those of the western National Park Service areas, notably Grand Canyon, Bryce Canyon and Grand Teton National Parks. The staff in all of the areas visited was most helpful.

Special appreciation goes to my wife, Janice, who spent more than a year at the drawing board, working on the illustrations.

Thanks go to Vinson Brown and Little, Brown and Company, Publishers, of Boston, Massachusetts, for the use of the plant drawings of Don Greame Kelley, originally published in the book, THE AMATEUR NATURALIST'S HANDBOOK, and used on page 296 of this book.

INTRODUCTION

This book is intended as a guide to edible plants. Do not leave it at home on the bookshelf, but take it along when you go into the field for hiking, camping or other outdoor activities.

The plants catalogued in this guide are found in the western third of the United States, that area bounded by the western border of the Great Plains, the Pacific Ocean, and the borders of Mexico and Canada. Many species which occur near the borders of Mexico and Canada are found for some distance into them, thus this guide may be of use in northwestern Mexico (including Baja California) and southwestern Canada.

As one whose professional and nonprofessional life has been spent studying the world of nature, I have always had an interest in edible plants. My interest has been sharpened, however, by curious observers who accidentally found me in the act of uprooting some dried-up edible, or attempting to photograph it. These people frequently were so interested in the subject that I often have been kept talking about the edible plants of that area for hours. In fact, the interest has been such that I finally decided to put the information I had into the form of a book.

Invariably a discussion concerning edible plants evolves to the matter of survival in the wilds. Many old wives' tales are told concerning survival in the out-of-doors. Many are completely true; some have only a grain of truth in them; others are completely false. One such tale is that a man lost in the woods need only watch the animals eat to find out what he can eat. Not true! Most squirrels, for example, can eat the deadly Amanita mushroom (not all species of Amanita are toxic, however) with no ill effect. According to Kingsbury's *Poisonous Plants of the United States and Canada,* an Amanita species is credited with a human mortality rate of between 50 and 90 percent. The Amanita victim who recovers must convalesce for a month, and escapes with no less than an enlarged liver.

It is often said that a pleasant taste ensures safety in eating an unknown plant. Water Hemlock (*Cicuta douglasii* and other species) is considered the most poisonous plant in the United States and Canada, having caused many fatalities over the years. Its roots smell and taste like parsnips, certainly not unpleasant to anyone liking parsnips! Furthermore, Water Hemlock sufficiently resembles several well known edible plants that fatal errors are often made.

Frequently one hears that to test for edibility one should eat only a small piece, wait for bad effects, and if none appear after a reasonable length of time, assume that the plant is edible. Only one root of Water Hemlock is needed to kill a cow, and a piece slightly larger than an ordinary peanut will kill a man.

It should be emphasized that one should never eat more than a very small quantity of an edible plant one is not accustomed to, even if it is positively identified. This writer never ceases to be amazed at what foolishness, or lack of good common sense, some people manifest in eating wild edible plants. There are not a few people that for some inexplicable reason will eat much more of a wild edible plant than they would of a domestic one. Never eat more of a wild edible plant, even if your digestive system is accustomed to that species, than you would of a comparable domestic edible plant. The layman is, in general, unaware of the fact that many *domestic* food plants can be poisonous—through improper preparation, excessive consumption, bad growing conditions, incorrect use of fertilizer, employment of certain pesticides and herbicides, choice of the wrong plant part, or for other reasons.

Common cultivated turnips, for example, contain a goiter-causing substance. Where turnips have been used as fodder for livestock, congenital goiter has appeared in lambs, and there is no reason to suppose it could not happen in humans if they were to eat turnips in the same relative amounts. Cultivated onions and wild onions are in the same genus, and all contain a poisonous alkaloid that can cause severe anemia when steadily eaten in large quantities, whether fresh or cooked. Why are people unaware of this? The answer is that long-standing cultural tradition usually limits the amount of a vegetable one eats.

Apple seeds contain dangerous amounts of hydrogen cyanide, and have caused numerous poisonings. To eat a few is safe, but there is a case on record of a man who, liking apple seeds, saved a cupful to eat all at one time. He died of cyanide poisoning. The ordinary domestic peach, any variety, contains hydrogen cyanide throughout the tree, but the nut-like seeds to be found within the pit are especially heavy in cyanide. Apricot seeds are also high in cyanide and have caused human death.

Quantities of raw, maturing, cultivated asparagus can cause poisoning. Many cultivated grains can become quite poisonous when infected with ergot (see Glossary). Lima beans contain hydrogen cyanide and have caused human poisoning. Ordinary cabbage contains a goiter-causing compound. Citrus fruit (orange, grapefruit, etc.) seeds have caused poisoning in livestock. Horseradish is quite poisonous, but because of its sharp flavor it is unlikely that anyone would eat enough of it to cause severe poisoning. Rhubarb is well known to have poisonous leaves that have caused human death. The list could go on—however, our purpose lies not in frightening the reader out of eating wholesome domestic vegetables, but in pointing out that reasonable common sense is needed in using *domestic* as well as *wild* plants. Domestic vegetables rarely poison people because they come from known sources, are eaten in well established, limited amounts, and are prepared properly.

The source of wild edibles, like the domestics, should be verified if one is to be safe in using plants from that source. Edible plants grown in one area may be perfectly safe, while the same species grown in another area may cause any of various forms of mineral poisoning. If unsure, eat only small quantities, gradually increasing your intake over a period of hours, or days. At the first sign of physical discomfort, cease eating the known edible from the unproven source. A discussion of the common types of mineral poisoning follows.

Nitrate and nitrite poisoning. An enormous number of wild and domestic plants can accumulate toxic levels of nitrates, usually the result of overfertilization. Wild edibles growing near cultivated fields should not be eaten unless you know that they are safe. Loss of livestock in these circumstances is common, and human poisoning has occurred. Symptoms vary, but include severe digestive upset, discolored urine, weakness, and trembling, and the skin may become bluish. Consult a doctor immediately and tell him of your suspicions, so that he can test for nitrate or nitrite poisoning, if deemed advisable, and treat accordingly.

Selenium poisoning. All of the western states include soils that, in localized areas, contain dangerous concentrations of selenium. The majority of plants are considered nonaccumulators of selenium, but there are some that will absorb it if it is present, and some that apparently must have it for best growth. If, however, selenium is in the soil in sufficient concentration, *most* plants can absorb toxic amounts. Often this affects the plant itself so that it looks diseased or stunted, but not all species react in this way, so the appearance of a plant is not a good indicator. Also, those plants that need selenium and those that will readily absorb it if present, can act as concentrator plants. By absorbing selenium from the soil, even soil that may have it in very low concentration, these plants can cause the ground under them and within a few feet around them to become high in selenium through leaf drop, or by dying and decaying in the soil. At some later time a "nonaccumulator" may grow in the spot once occupied by the concentrator plant, and thus become poisonous. Or, a nonaccumulator may grow within a few feet of a concentrator, and become poisonous. Domestic plants as well as wild ones can be affected. Corn, wheat, oats, barley and vegetable crops have been known to absorb toxic amounts of selenium.

The symptoms in humans vary with the form and amount of the dose ingested, but they include loss of appetite, mental depression, difficulty in breathing, excessive urine production, a weak and rapid pulse, kidney

swelling and pain, blurry vision, weakness, digestive upset, and eventually coma, with death occurring because
of respiratory and heart muscle failure.

Plant genera that are listed in this book and that could
cause selenium poisoning are:

Obligate: Those plants that need selenium for best
growth thereby tending to indicate the presence of the
element in the soil.

> *Stanleya,* all species   Prince's Plume

Facultative: Those plants that will absorb selenium if
it be present, but do not need it, and therefore do not
necessarily indicate the presence of selenium in the soil.

Aster spp.	Aster
Atriplex spp.	Saltbushes
Castilleja spp.	Paintbrushes
Commandra pallida	Bastard Toadflax
Grindelia spp.	Gumweeds

Of the plants which are considered nonedible, and
which therefore are not listed in this book, all of the
many species of *Astragalus* are considered to be selenium
indicators, and it would be a good idea to learn the appearance of this genus as a whole, which would aid in
identifying seleniferous soils. An excellent reference for
doing this is Abrams, *Illustrated Flora of the Pacific
States,* Volume II, starting on page 569.

Remember, though, that even if *Astragalus* be present,
whatever selenium may be in the soil often is in such low
concentration that the nonaccumulators are not poisonous, nor possibly the indicators, either. Certainly this
must explain how Southwestern Indians and early settlers used Prince's Plume, which modern biology says is
a selenium indicator.

*Copper, lead, cadmium poisoning. Herbicide, fungi-
cide, pesticide poisoning.* There was a day when poisoning by the items mentioned in this heading was of no
concern. Those days are long gone. Wherever you go in
the West you must bear in mind the possibility that
plants may be made poisonous through the deposition
on or in their tissues of various compounds produced as
industrial waste. Usually, but not always, the source of
such pollution is nearby and obvious. Unless you are

certain that the dusty edible plants you have found are covered with harmless fine soil particles, do not eat them, for the dust may be toxic industrial pollution, or the results of a spray designed to "control" something in the environment.

Plants along heavily traveled highways have been known to contain toxic amounts of lead, the source of which is the lead compound used in gasoline. In areas where copper sulphate has been used for many years as a fungicide, the absorbed copper in the vegetation has reached toxic levels. Commercial superphosphate fertilizers contain cadmium as an impurity, and it is absorbed by the plants. Cadmium is known to accumulate in the mammalian body. Since humans are good examples of mammals, cadmium accumulation is a potential danger.

Then there are the legions of organic herbicides, fungicides and pesticides around which there is much controversy as to their dangers. In my view, which may or may not be scientific but seems to me to be supported by common sense, any compound capable of killing any living organism, or any part of a living organism, or capable of changing the normal physiological processes of any living organism, offers, at the very least, potential harm to all living things. In spite of the various claims made, real harm to warm-blooded creatures by various pesticides has occurred—even as far away as Antarctica. In spite of various claims made, many of the elements and compounds found in herbicides, fungicides and pesticides are poisonous not only to man but to thousands of kinds of other organisms not intended as targets for killing. Despite the claims of various manufacturers, no one yet has made an herbicide, fungicide or pesticide that is 100% specific for *one* organism.

What is worse, distance and isolation from the haunts of mankind are no guarantee whatever that somebody has not polluted the local environment. In one of the West's most isolated mountain ranges—a range no nearer anywhere than fifty miles to a paved road—I myself have seen an airplane spraying a defoliant on the brush. The application, of course, was totally indiscriminate—everything in the plane's wake dripped with defoliant spray

Many of the shrubs and other plant species were edible in some way.

The only way to be safe is to talk to people who have eaten from the wild plants of your chosen area with no ill effects, and, even then, remember to eat only small amounts until you are sure your body will accept the new diet.

Attention should be called to the indexes in the back of this book. In addition to the general index listing common and scientific names, there are two other indexes, one of which compiles the food uses as to type for quick reference, the other of which lists the nonfood uses to which many of these plants may be put. A major portion of this last-mentioned index refers to the medicinal qualities of many of the plants listed in this book. It should be noted that while a few of these plants have been tried, and proven to contain valuable drugs used in treating various disorders, the vast majority of plants have only presumed curative powers. Folk medicines should always, at best, be approached very cautiously. Morever, where the plants do contain useful drugs no attempt is made in this book to give adequate instructions for either the preparation or the use of the drug. Such information as is listed is given for interest only. As with practically anything, overuse or misuse of a folk medicine could result in harm to the body.

On harvesting wild edible plants: A growing number of people feel that the world is grossly overpopulated. Whatever your point of view on world population, one thing can be said for sure: there are too many people living in the Western United States (or almost anywhere else, for that matter) for anyone, even one person, to go into the so-called wilds and live off the fat of the land. The land is not fat. The information in this book was not set down so that the reader could walk along a trail irresponsibly harvesting the wild edible plants. The information collected herein was recorded because there was danger that much of it would eventually be lost. Even now, a good deal of the material contained in this book is not available anywhere else. Yet a great many of the plants listed herein are nutritious, and superior in flavor to our convential domesticated plants, making the temptation to overcollect them almost overwhelming. Furthermore, quite obviously, none of them have been bred or overfertilized to "outgrow" themselves for the sake of a good appearance in the supermarket, a practice which many feel results in a decrease of nutritive quality in many domestic plants.

In consideration of the fact that our wild edibles should not be harvested wholesale it should be realized by the reader that many of these plants are easily cultivated in the garden. Seeds, a few roots or portions thereof, slips, suckers, etc., can be collected and grown to produce many more, so that the wild stock is not depleted. Many of these plants, in fact, are more easily grown than domestic ones because they are native and better adapted for withstanding native pests and the climate.

Having enumerated the foregoing cautions, let me again remind the reader to thoroughly learn the identification of the wild edible plants he collects, and to employ some common sense in their use.

Another popular but dangerous maxim is to know only those plants that are poisonous, because everything else is edible. To acquire knowledge of all the known poisonous plants in the West would be as formidable a task as to have ready knowledge of all the known edible plants. Moreover, only a small percentage of the more than 12,000 species of plants found in the West is known to be either edible *or* poisonous. There are literally thousands about which we know nothing. The list of poisonous and edible plants lengthens as further information is collected. For survival or other purposes, it is simply best to know specifically what is edible.

There are a number of reasons why people look first to plants to provide a meal from our natural supply. First, plants are nearly always available and second, there is usually no food prejudice when it comes to eating a plant. Actually, insects are about as available as plants, but most people would not think of eating an insect.

Food prejudice and ignorance are the two primary reasons that people starve in the wilderness. Not long ago several hunters became lost in the vast wilderness of northern British Columbia. They starved to death in a pine forest composed of trees whose inner bark was not only edible, but rather nourishing. They also had available to them several species of white grubworms in the shallow soil and decaying logs. Admittedly, a fat, juicy grubworm is not easy to eat. For those whose palate rejects such food sources, this book will be of great value.

The material in this book was obtained for the most part by word of mouth during my travels through the West. Much data also came from widely scattered spots in various published and unpublished works. There are several good books and pamphlets available on edible plants, and these are listed in the Selected References; none, however, offer anywhere near as extensive coverage of the West as this guide. I have photographed several hundred of these plants throughout the West and have sampled at least one species from most of the genera presented.

Approximately 2000 species of edible plants classified in 307 genera are treated. In a number of instances the entire genus is edible. In such cases, the genus is treated as a single entry rather than by species. The illustration accompanying such an entry is that of one of the most palatable and/or common species of that genus. Naturally there are many genera in which only one plant is edible; in such instances, only that species is described. For large genera (one contains over 100 species!) consult a good flora of the area (see Selected References).

This survey is limited to the higher plants. No mushrooms are included because mushrooms are not particularly nourishing, many are difficult to identify positively, and there are a number of good mushroom guides available. Algae have also been excluded for although many algae are edible, most have an unbearably bad taste, are difficult for the layman to identify positively, and some are toxic, notably certain members of the bluegreen group.

There are hundreds of plants not listed in this book that were, or still are, used by western Indians and settlers. These plants can be classified according to their use: fiber plants, soap plants, medicinal plants, fish poisons, dye plants, gum plants and tobacco plants, in addition to edible plants. The inclusion of all of these plants in this book would make it too large to be of practical use.

Although the main purpose in this book is the discussion of the edible qualities of western plants, other uses for plants have been included because of some particular interest. No medicinal plants have been listed except a select few whose prepared medicine is nourishing and could be used as food.

The material is presented in as abbreviated a form as is consistent with completeness. The nomenclature used by Munz and Keck in *A California Flora* has been followed where possible to provide consistency.

MAJOR PLANT AREAS IN THE WEST

Knowledge of the major plant areas of the West not only broadens a person's perspective of his environment and facilitates location and identification of edible plants, but as the reader gains experience in the field, he will learn that each major habitat is characterized by a set of edible plants. Hence, whenever that habitat is encountered in that area, the same set of plants may be anticipated, although major habitats may have somewhat different geographic areas. Considerable work has been done on plant areas of the West, and there is some conflict of opinion concerning the extent of the areas in question and which plant actually dominates.

Only a very general view of the diversity of plant cover that is found in the West is given here. For more detailed information refer to books listed in *Selected References.*

Americans are so mentally oriented to their state boundaries that the major plant covers or types are here presented by state, with the states placed in commonly accepted geographical groupings.

NORTHWEST

Washington: Slightly over one-third of the western part of the state is covered with a forest cover that is typically called by such names as Pacific Conifer Forest, Pacific Temperate Rain Forest, etc. Except for areas under cultivation, this forest reaches from the coast nearly to the crest of the Cascade Mountains where it encounters a narrow strip of subalpine forest. The lower area is one of large trees, some reaching 300 feet in height. Douglas fir, western hemlock, western red cedar and a few other common trees compose the Pacific Conifer Forest. The ground cover is dense with shrubs and herbaceous plants.

On the east slope of the Cascades, there is a ponderosa pine forest. This extends south the entire length of the state and eastward across the northern third. Other tree species, such as the lodgepole pine, are found sometimes covering many acres in the ponderosa forests.

The large southeastern corner of Washington, comprising over one-fourth of the state, is of native grassland ringing an extensive tract of sagebrush except where the land is today cultivated. There is also a small ponderosa area in this part of the state.

Washington does not contain large areas of subalpine forest, but a small strip is found running most of the length of the Cascade crest. A small area is also found in the higher reaches of the mountainous Olympic Peninsula. Another small area occurs in the northeastern corner adjacent to Idaho. One of the most common trees found in the subalpine forest is the western white pine. A number of spruce and fir species occur here also.

Oregon: The western third of Oregon has almost the same forest complex as western Washington. The Willamette Valley is largely free of this forest for various reasons, one of the most important being that much of the land is used as farmland. There are some redwood trees on the extreme southwestern coast of Oregon. A more arid forest land, consisting primarily of sugar, ponderosa, and other pine species, exists in the southern fourth of western Oregon.

In the north central part of the state there is a large area of native grassland, an extension of the Washington grassland. Much of this is now under cultivation.

The east slope of the Cascades is covered with ponderosa pine for the entire length of the state. Ponderosa and other pines cover a large portion of the northeast quarter of Oregon in the Blue and Wallowa Mountains and extend south to meet with high sagebrush desert. A small area of subalpine cover is found in the Wallowa Mountains.

The Cascade crest of Oregon is covered with the same sort of subalpine forest as exists in Washington. This forest type extends south only three-fourths of the state, and then gives way to ponderosa and sugar pine forest.

High sagebrush desert covers most of the southeastern fourth of Oregon. This is the typical plant cover of the Great Basin, an area where there is no drainage to the sea.

In the almost exact center of Oregon there is a large tract of juniper forest. This forest is typically an open one with sage growing between the trees. Smaller areas of juniper appear in the high sage desert wherever proper conditions exist.

SOUTHWEST

California: The northern California coast is characterized by a narrow strip of redwood forest running from Oregon south to the Golden Gate, and with extensions in Santa Cruz and Monterey Counties to the south. Outside the redwood area, there is a southward extension of Oregon's Pacific Conifer Forest, with the Douglas Fir a dominant tree.

In the north central part of California, the sugar-ponderosa pine forest that started in Oregon continues southward through the Coast Range on the west to San Francisco Bay and on the east down the western slope of the Sierra Nevada Mountains for over two-thirds the length of the state. Digger pine and other, more dryland species enter into this forest about one-fourth of the distance south.

In the northeast corner is a large area of ponderosa pine similar to that of Oregon. This extends south along the east slope of the Cascade-Sierra Nevada ranges to about the middle of California.

Eastward, the ponderosa is bordered by a narrow strip of juniper. Pinon pine enters the southern portion of this juniper strip. Large areas of juniper and pinon are found in the Inyo-White Mountain area northwest of Death Valley.

In the extreme northeast corner, there is a westward extension of the high sagebrush desert of Nevada. There is also some sage in the valleys of the Inyo-White Mountain range and in the Owens Valley.

Originally the great Central Valley of California was covered with various bunch grasses and contained many square miles of marsh land. Now, because of agriculture and over-grazing, most of this original cover has disappeared and the swamps largely drained, to be replaced by cultivated lands and pasture.

Bordering the Central Valley is a narrow strip of chaparral which meets the ponderosa pine forest on both slopes. Chaparral is also found extensively covering the south coast ranges from Monterey to Mexico. Belts of oaks, such as live oak and black oak, are common in the foothills outside of the desert, cultivated and coniferous areas.

The southeastern fourth of the state includes the Mojave and Colorado deserts. These are hot, dry areas characterized by creosote bush, shadscale, and other desert plants such as the joshua tree and cholla cacti. This desert extends across the Colorado River through southwestern Arizona into Mexico.

Subalpine areas in California are not large. A narrow strip runs through the higher reaches of the Sierra Nevada and some small areas are found in Lassen Volcanic National Park. A rather large area occurs in the center of California's Klamath Ranges.

Nevada: This state is characteristically thought of as being nothing but high sagebrush desert. Admittedly, Nevada probably has more square miles of sage than any other state. This plant type extends from Oregon and Idaho over the entire state except for the southern tip bordering California and Arizona. This southern portion is covered with the same sort of creosote bush and cactus desert as is California's Mojave Desert.

It should be noted that Nevada has rather large areas of juniper-pinon forest spread throughout the state. These forests are found on the slopes of the many north-south oriented mountain ranges spaced over Nevada. Some of these ranges reach a height sufficient to trap enough moisture to support ponderosa pine and even some spruce, fir and aspen. One of the most notable of these ranges is the Snake Range in eastern Nevada which includes 13,063-foot Wheeler Peak. This area even supports a bristlecone pine forest in a subalpine region.

Arizona: The northwest and northeast corners of the state support a southward extension of the Great Basin sagebrush desert. The Kaibab Plateau north of the Grand Canyon is ringed extensively by juniper and pinon. Huge forests of pinon and juniper extend from the south rim of the Grand Canyon almost continuously southeast to the end of the Mogollon Mesa and south into Mexico. The southeastern pinon-juniper forest of Arizona is much broken with native grassland.

A beautiful forest of ponderosa covers the Kaibab Plateau and the Mogollon Mesa, and a fairly large tract is found in the northeastern corner of Arizona in the Chuska Mountain area.

The large southwestern one-third to one-half of the state is covered with the same type of creosote bush desert as is found in southeastern California; it extends into Mexico. Certain areas of this desert are famous for their cactus varieties, notably the saguaro, organ pipe, barrel and jumping cholla cacti. Small areas in the mountains of the central south and south-east have oak woods and chaparral cover.

Utah: This state is rather neatly bisected on a north-south axis by mountain ranges covered on their lower slopes with juniper and pinon. In the higher areas there are ponderosa pine forests and many small forests of a nearly subalpine variety, containing spruce and firs.

The Unita Mountains just south of the Wyoming border are part of the Rocky Mountain complex and have a flora characteristic of that region. In these mountains are found the only large areas of subalpine forest in Utah. Juniper and pinon are scattered throughout western and southeastern Utah wherever conditions permit. Some ponderosa forests are found in the Abajo Mountains of southeastern Utah.

Large areas of sage are found in western and south-eastern Utah.

Extensive enough to mention is the Great Salt Lake Desert, much of which supports a saltbush cover. A large expanse of this desert, however, is almost pure crystalline salt in which nothing will grow.

New Mexico and extreme western Texas: The north-western corner of New Mexico contains a sagebrush region similar to that of the Great Basin. Much of the eastern part of the state is native grassland, in what is called the *Staked Plains.*

There are large areas of juniper and pinon in the lower mountain and plateau areas through the central part of New Mexico from Colorado into Texas. Extensive forests of this type are also found in the western part of the state.

The mountainous north-central area, western sectors and the Sacramento Mountains of the south-central region contain extensive ponderosa pine forests.

The Sangre de Christo Mountains of north-central New Mexico have a fairly large subalpine forest. More subalpine can be seen in scattered high mountains of western New Mexico and a small area of subalpine occurs in the Sacramento Mountains.

The Chihuahuan Desert extends through extreme western Texas into southern New Mexico and is much broken in Texas by hills covered by pinon and juniper type forest.

In the extreme southwestern corner of New Mexico there is native grassland broken by hills containing juniper and pinon and also some chaparral and oak woods.

THE ROCKY MOUNTAIN STATES

Colorado: Over one-third of the eastern part of the state is, or once was, native prairie grassland.

Most of the mountainous western half of Colorado is covered with a narrow band of juniper and pinon at the lower elevations becoming ponderosa pine forest at higher elevations, and eventually gives way to subalpine forests in the high mountains. Above this there are rather extensive alpine areas, but these are relatively unimportant to the collector of edible plants.

The northwestern and extreme southwestern corners of Colorado are sagebrush desert.

Wyoming: Much of eastern Wyoming is native grassland. Ponderosa pine (and other species) forest is found in the Black Hills, the Larame Range, Bighorn Mountains and the Medicine Bow Mountains.

Nearly all of southwestern Wyoming is high sagebrush desert.

The northwestern corner of Wyoming is the well-known Grand Teton-Yellowstone area. Here are found extensive areas of ponderosa, Douglas fir and subalpine forest. Some subalpine areas are found in the Bighorn Mountains as well.

Idaho: Most of the southern third of Idaho is high sagebrush desert. Fairly extensive forests of juniper are found in hilly southwestern Idaho, south of the Snake

River. Small areas of ponderosa and related tree types occur at the higher elevations in the Owyhee Range of southwestern Idaho. A ponderosa pine type forest occurs along the eastern border of Idaho and Wyoming southward to Utah. The southeast corner of the state contains some fairly large ponderosa forests with Douglas fir and other species in the higher mountain reaches.

The northern half of Idaho, stretching to Canada, supports a flora typical of the Rocky Mountains with some Pacific Coast elements. There are large areas of ponderosa pine, western larch, Douglas fir, white pine, other species of pine and fir and large areas of typical subalpine forest.

Rather extensive lodgepole pine forests occur in mountainous central Idaho and in the northeastern corner adjacent to Wyoming and Montana.

Montana: The eastern two-thirds of Montana is largely prairie and not covered in this book.   The mountainous western third is part of the Rocky Mountain chain.   Although there are large areas of grassland in southwestern Montana, they are of quite different aspect than the eastern prairie.

Large lodgepole pine forests, with subalpine forest coming in at the higher elevations, are found in the western portion of the state. An extensive ponderosa pine forest is found in the southern half of the Cabinet Mountains.

Western Montana also supports many square miles of spruce-fir forest.

HOW TO USE THIS BOOK

Before attempting to use this book in the field, the reader should become thoroughly familiar with its organization and should study some of the entries. As the reader becomes familiar with the book, it will become of greater value to him.

The entries have been arranged according to their natural distribution within geographical areas. This method of grouping allows the reader to gain a quick idea of what to look for wherever he is in the West: he need only consult the chapter on *Plants Found*

Throughout the West and the chapter pertaining to the area he is in for a complete list of edible plants in his area.

Each entry is described under the geographical area of its greatest abundance. Each plant is numbered and the number given with the illustration. The scientific name of each entry is given first and the common name, if any, is listed just beneath. Scientific names are more accurate than common names, since for a single plant there may be several common names that change with location. Directly after the scientific name, a number in parenthesis indicates the number of edible species in the genus being described. Those species that are not edible are mentioned. For each entry there is a brief summary of that plant's distribution in the West; most plants are found in regions other than the one under which they are described, for very few of these plants are confined to one area. Perhaps there are more plants confined to the desert of southwestern Arizona than any of the other three regions of the West.

In each of the descriptive chapters, the plants are arranged by genus and the genera placed in families in the same order as in Munz and Keck, *A California Flora.* Numbered illustrations are put on separate pages so that the reader can practice naming them by looking at each picture and seeing if he or she can guess the correct name. This practice will make recognition quicker in the field.

After a plant has been found in the field, it should be identified positively before it is eaten, because similar species may be toxic. For example, the edible cow parsnip *(Heracleum lanatum)* resembles the death-dealing water hemlock *(Cicuta species),* an introduced European plant that is found widely spread over the West.

Some plants should be eaten sparingly at first since the body must accustom itself to them. One such plant is the bearberry honeysuckle *(Lonicera involucrata)* which is said to contain saponin, a soapy and somewhat poisonous substance. The Indians used the pleasant-tasting fruit of this plant whenever they desired and suffered no ill effects.

There are mixed opinions concerning the edibility of some plants. The blue elderberries *(Sambucus species)* for example, are said to be completely safe, and these species are used extensively for wine, jelly and pie making. The red elderberries, other species of the same genus, are nearly always said to be poisonous, yet the author has come upon a number of people who insist that they "eat the red ones all the time and never get sick." However that may be, the red species are not included in this book as being edible.

Some plants included in this book, such as the California Buckeye *(Aesculis californica)*, are definitely toxic in the natural state. Only through special preparation methods do such plants and their products become edible. It is therefore wise to follow the directions for preparation explicitly.

The reader will find frequent use of such words as boiled, steamed, potherb, salad plant, beverage, meal, mush, etc. These words are defined and discussed in the glossary at the back of the book along with various botanical terms that have been necessary for plant descriptions. They refer mainly to various uses to which a plant may be put. The reader should also understand that nearly all of these plants can be prepared in as many ways as his ingenuity can devise. The mark of a good cook is the personal touch in the use of spices and seasonings.

PLANTS FOUND THROUGHOUT THE WEST

This group of plants is the largest of the four geographically designated groups. The reason is paradoxical. The climate and topography of the West are extremely diverse between different areas, yet there are large regions with sufficient uniformity within each area to support a relatively uniform plant cover. Moreover, these plants, probably through greater adaptability, are able to adjust to whatever environmental extremes exist.

The fact that there are many edible plants found virtually everywhere is gratifying. Wherever one travels in the West, he can expect to find these same useful plants.

Also listed here are a number of plants that are not found completely throughout the West, but have a distribution sufficiently extensive to be included in this chapter.

1. *Equisetum* species (5) (Horsetail Family)
   Horsetails, Foxtail, Rush, Scouring Rush, Joint-Grass

   Preparation and Uses: The tough outer tissue can be peeled away and the sweet pulp eaten raw. Indians and early settlers used the silicon-covered stems to scour out pots and pans. Many campers do this today. Horsetails are known to have poisoned livestock and should probably be eaten sparingly. There have been no reported cases of human poisoning from eating the rindless pulp.

   Habitat and Distribution: Horsetails are found in moist soil along streams and rivers, in marshes and other damp habitats nearly throughout the West.

   Description: These often branching plants are rushlike, with creeping, perennial, branching rootstocks, rooted at the nodes. The aerial stems may be annual or perennial, are cylindrical, fluted, simple or with whorled branches at the jointed nodes. The internodes are usually hollow. The surfaces of the stems are covered with silica. The cones are terminal.

2. *Pteridium aquilinum* (1) (Fern Order)
    Bracken, Brake Fern

Preparation and Uses: The young fronds may be eaten raw or cooked and are at their best when still shaped like fiddlenecks. Only the tender parts should be gathered, rubbed to remove the wool, washed, and boiled about an hour in salted water until quite tender, or they may be salted and steamed. The starchy rootstocks (rhizomes) may be eaten roasted or boiled, but they usually remain quite tough. Close relatives of this native fern are used in a similar manner from New Zealand to Europe.

Brake Fern has long been known to fatally poison livestock that arc fed large quantities of it over fairly long periods of time. Although there is no record of human death from similar conditions, no doubt people using excessive amounts of the fern over lengthy periods of time would also eventually be poisoned. It has recently been demonstrated that the whole fern plant contains a powerful carcinogen, readily causing stomach cancer in livestock and experimental animals. Again, this has not been linked to any human deaths from stomach cancer, and, again, the animals were fed enormous amounts over a long period of time. Nevertheless, in spite of its long and worldwide history of human use, dating back at least as far as that of water cress, *P. aquilinum* is a species that should be used with caution.

Habitat and Distribution: Brake Fern is found in fields, burns, moist rich woods, and rocky canyons throughout the West. It is not found in desert areas.

Description: The plant is a coarse fern with long, creeping, woody, branched, hairy rhizomes and solitary fronds. The large, pinnately compound, 3-divided fronds are stout and erect to reclining, with a feltlike covering near the base.

3. *Pseudotsuga menziesii* (1) (Pine Family)
Douglas Fir

Preparation and Uses: The fresh needles may be steeped in hot water to make a palatable, refreshing tea said to be high in vitamin C.

The Douglas Fir was extensively used by northwestern Indians for lumber, fish harpoon shafts and other implements. The pliable roots of this and other conifers were used in weaving baskets.

Habitat and Distribution: The Douglas Fir is a forest tree of the more moist areas of the West.

Description: The tree is a conical, evergreen conifer with long whorled branches and drooping twigs. The gray bark is usually deeply furrowed. The petioled needles are flat, grooved, dark green above, lighter green below, and usually spreading all around the stem like the bristles of a bottle brush. The small cone has characteristic 3-tongued scales.

4. *Juniperus* species (8) (Pine Family)
Juniper, Cedar

Preparation and Uses: All of the species produce edible berries although some are more palatable than others, notably *J. deppeana*. The so-called berries are best when dried, ground into meal, and prepared as mush or cakes, but they may be eaten raw.

The wood is used commercially in manufacturing lead pencils and for fence posts. The berries of *J. communis* produce the oil of juniper, much used in patent medicines, and which gives the characteristic flavor to gin.

Habitat and Distribution: The Juniper is one of the most characteristic trees of the West, forming large areas of woodland throughout the more arid portions. It is found in pure stands toward the

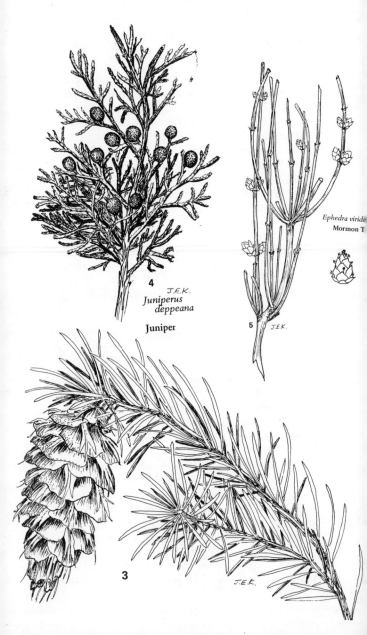

J.E.K.
Juniperus deppeana

Juniper

4

Ephedra viridi
Mormon T

5   J.E.K.

3   J.E.K.

north and commonly occurs in conjunction with the pinon pine in Colorado, Nevada, Utah, New Mexico, Arizona and California.

Description: These evergreen plants range from low spreading shrubs with rather needle-like leaves to fairly good-sized trees with scale-like leaves. The aromatic bark is often thin, soft, fibrous and shreddy, (used by Indians for baby's diapers). Probably the best way to identify the tree is by the aromatic blue to blue-green berry-like cones.

5. *Ephedra* species (8) (Ephedra Family)
Mormon Tea, Brigham Tea, Teamster Tea, Desert Tea, Joint Fir

Preparation and Uses: All of the species make good tea, although some are better than others. Place in boiling water a handful of green or dry leaves and stems for each cup of tea desired. Remove the brew immediately from the fire and allow it to steep for 20 minutes or more, depending on individual taste. To bring out the full flavor, a teaspoon of sugar per cup should be added along with some lemon juice or strawberry jam. A surprising number of people in northern Arizona, southern Utah, and eastern Nevada do this today.

The small, hard, brown seeds may be ground and used as a bitter meal, or added to white bread dough to flavor it.

The Indians and early white settlers used a very strong tea of the plant for the treatment of syphilis and other diseases, and as a tonic. The drug ephedrine is extracted from a Chinese species, *E. sinica,* and commonly used as a mild substitute for adrenalin and as an astringent.

Habitat and Distribution: Mormon Tea is found in desert, grassland, and sage country, generally in the more arid areas of California, Nevada, Arizona, Oregon, Utah, New Mexico, Wyoming, Colorado, and southern Idaho.

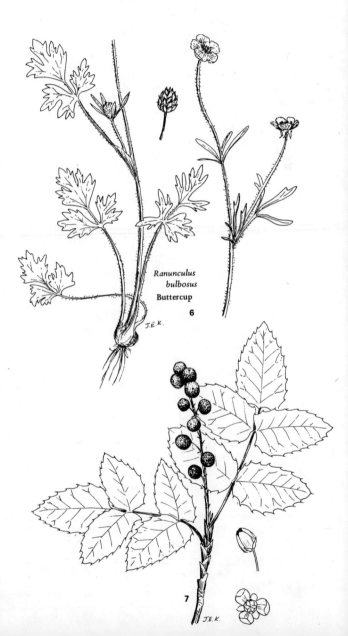

Ranunculus bulbosus
Buttercup

6

7

Description: These plants are stiff shrubs, with slender, jointed, stiff, opposite or whorled branches marked with fine longitudinal lines. The leaves are reduced to scales, and are paired, or arranged in threes. The flowers are conelike, the staminate flowers bearing 2 to 8 or more stamens. The hard, brown seeds number 1 to 3.

6. *Ranunculus* species (35) (Buttercup Family)
   Buttercup, Crowfoot

Preparation and Uses: All of the Buttercups are more or less poisonous when raw. Toxicity depends on species, amount eaten, state of growth, and the conditions under which the plant grew.

According to Kingsbury, the poisonous principle is a volatile yellow oil called protoanemonin. It may be removed from the plants by thorough cooking. If any acid taste remains, spit out the mouthful, and recook the plants in fresh water.

Western Indians parched the seeds, ground them into meal, and made bread. The roots were boiled and eaten, and the foliage of some, such as *R. repens* (an early introduction from the Old World and now established in the West) contain little protoanemonin and were easily rendered safe by thorough boiling. *R. bulbosus* (also an Old World native) is one of the best in providing edible roots. Early western settlers pickled the young flowers. Some Indian groups obtained a yellow dye by crushing and washing the flowers.

It has been reported by some authors that the bulbs of *R. bulbosus* which have wintered over are mild enough to eat raw in the spring, but this is probably risky.

Habitat and Distribution: The many species range from moist to dry, shady to open habitats throughout the West. Probably it is safe to say that the majority live in open, reasonably moist ground.

Description: The Buttercups are common annual or perennial herbs with entire, cleft, irregularly toothed to divided or compound, alternate, often largely basal leaves. The roots vary from fibrous to fleshy and thick, or tuberous. The usually 5-petaled flowers are mostly yellow, but some are white, and a few may be red. The small, hard seeds are clustered on the receptacle, and have a hook or beak on them.

7. *Berberis* species (18) (Barberry Family)
    Barberry, Oregon Grape, Mahonia

Preparation and Uses: A number of species in this genus produce juicy berries which are pleasantly acid to the taste and make good pies and jellies. A brilliant yellow dye may be obtained by boiling the roots and bark.

Some of the species, perhaps all, contain in their roots berberine, a yellow crystalline alkaloid which is used as a tonic and antiperiodic.

Habitat and Distribution: The Barberry is found in woods and thickets in mountains throughout the West.

Description: The plants are large to small shrubs; the wood and inner bark are yellow. The leaves are evergreen, alternate, simple or compound, prickly, thick, and smooth. When compound, the leaflets number 3 to many. The flowers are yellow. The sepals, petals and stamens each number 6.

8. *Brasenia schreberi* (1) (Water-lily Family)
    Water Shield

Preparation and Uses: The tuberous roots are starchy and may be peeled, boiled and eaten, or dried and stored, or ground into flour. The unexpanded leaves and leaf stems may be eaten in salad, slime and all.

Habitat and Distribution: Water Shield is found

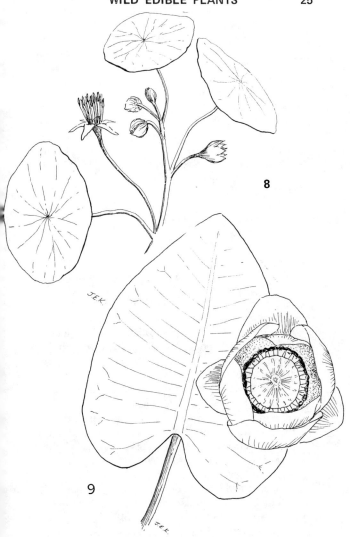

8

9

in ponds and ditches throughout the greater portion of the West. It is not officially listed in Arizona and Colorado, but should be looked for in those states. This single species is native to a wide area of the world, including North America, Asia, Africa and Australia.

Description: Water Shield is an aquatic plant with slender, branching stems. The leaves are entire, floating, oval to elliptic in shape, green above, often purple beneath, long-stemmed, and have the stalk or petiole attached to the lower surface instead of the base or edge. The small, purple flowers have sepals and petals that are similar to each other.

9. *Nuphar polysepalum* (1) (Water-lily Family)
   Yellow Pond Lily

Preparation and Uses: The globular seed vessels become full grown in late July and August and may be collected with their seeds. When dry, the seeds are easily removed and will keep indefinitely. The seeds are delicious when placed in a frying pan on an open fire, or on a hot stove until they swell and pop open. The popped seeds resemble popcorn in appearance and taste, and may then be eaten or ground into meal.

The tubers or roots are excellent eating and have a core rich in starch. The tubers may be boiled or roasted after which they may be easily peeled and the core eaten as is or placed in soup or stew. The plant is best prepared when the root is peeled, the core dried, ground into meal, and used as flour. The tubers have a sweetish taste.

Habitat and Distribution: The Yellow Pond Lily is found in lakes, ponds, and slow moving streams from Alaska into California and Colorado.

Description: This plant is easily recognized in its habitat by its large, floating leaves which are 4 to 14 inches across, and its beautiful yellow flowers that are up to 5 inches across.

10. *Malva neglecta* and related species (7)
(Mallow Family)
Mallow, Orange Mallow, Cheese-Weed

Preparation and Uses: The leaves and stems of all the species may be boiled as a green, but *M. neglecta* is the most flavorful. However, this is one of those plants that requires some getting used to. Large amounts should not be eaten at any one time for it will cause a digestive disorder.

Habitat and Distribution: The various species are found in waste places, roadsides, and desert lands throughout the West.

Description: These plants are biennial or annual, sparsely hairy, or nearly hairless. The leaves are flat and of circular outline, or kidney-shaped. The flowers, though small, are showy with white, pink, or orange petals.

11. *Sidalcea neomexicana* (1) (Mallow Family)
Prairie Mallow, Checkermallow, False Mallow

Preparation and Uses: The plant is edible cooked as greens.

Habitat and Distribution: Prairie Mallow is frequent in wet meadows, along streams, and in wet, alkaline soil throughout the West.

Description: This is a perennial, herbaceous plant, 1 to 3 feet tall, with woody roots. The branches may be erect or sprawling at the base. The palmate, circular, basal leaves are toothed, with the teeth rounded to shallowly lobed at the apex. The purple-rose to white flowers are borne in a raceme.

12. *Erodium cicutarium* (1) (Geranium Family)
Herons Bill, Alfilarea, Storkbill

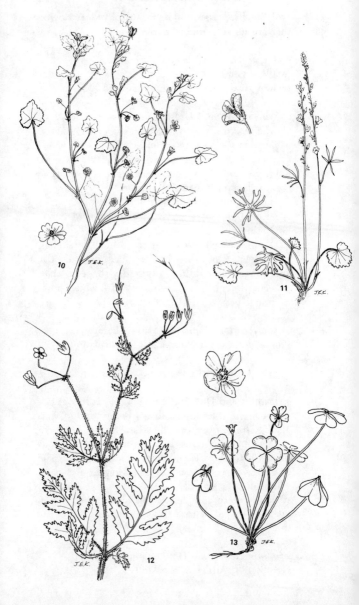

Preparation and Uses: The young plants may be used in salad or cooked as potherbs. Herons Bill is an important winter and early spring forage for livestock on open range.

Habitat and Distribution: The plant is found in open places, moist or dry, through the West.

Description: Herons Bill is an herb with prostrate, spreading stems, forming mats. The 2-10 rose to lavender flowers are on somewhat glandular stalks that are covered with short, soft hairs. The seed pods resemble a heron's or stork's bill.

13. *Oxalis oregana* and related species (16) (Oxalis or Wood Sorrel Family)
    Wood Sorrel, Sheep Sorrel, Sourgrass, Redwood Sorrel

Preparation and Uses: The leaves and stems may be eaten raw or a mass of them allowed to ferment slightly to make a tasty dessert. The leaves may be mixed with other greens in a salad. It is said that the early pioneers of Oregon and Washington made a sort of rhubarb pie from the sour stems. The plants contain a high percentage of oxalic acid and should be eaten sparingly until one is accustomed to them.

Habitat and Distribution: Wood Sorrel is found in shady, moist habitats throughout the West.

Description: *Oxalis* is often mistaken for some kind of clover because of its clover-like leaf. All of the species are small herbs with long-petioled, palmately trifoliate leaves. The flowers are solitary, or like an umbel, and are yellow, pinkish, rose, white, or lilac in color. Sepals and petals number 5, the petals often being united near the base. Stamens number 10.

14. *Floerkea proserpinacoides* (1) (False Mermaid Family)
    False Mermaid

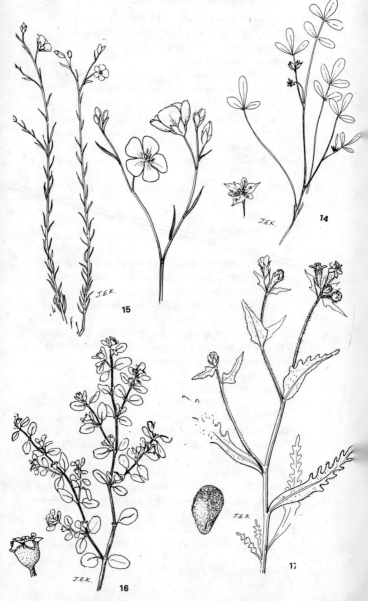

Preparation and Uses: The entire plant above ground may be eaten raw and makes a good salad. It is extremely tender and has a spicy flavor.

Habitat and Distribution: The plant is found in moist places throughout the West, except, apparently, in Arizona and New Mexico.

Description: False Mermaid is an inconspicuous, delicate, annual herb with alternate, divided leaves. The white flowers have 3 parts, and contain 6 stamens.

15. *Linum perenne* (ssp.) and *lewisii*
    (1) (Flax Family)
    Wild Flax, Prairie Flax, Blue Flax

Preparation and Uses: The Indians used the seeds roasted, dried and ground, or cooked with other foods. The seeds are high in oil content. The seeds contain cyanide and should not be eaten raw, but are safe after cooking. Although no cases of human poisoning have been recorded, poisoning has occurred in livestock.

The stems contain the fiber known as flax. *L. usitatissimum* is one species much cultivated for flax, from which linen is made, and for its seed, from which linseed oil is expressed.

Habitat and Distribution: Wild Flax is widely distributed throughout the West in dry ground.

Description: The plant is a slender herb with sky blue, rarely white, flowers on slender stems. The flowers open in the morning and usually close in the afternoon. Sepals, petals, and stamens are 5 in number. The leaves are entire, sessile, narrow, and so numerous as to almost cover the stem. Several stems arise from a somewhat woody base.

16. *Euphorbia serpyllifolia* (1) (Spurge Family)
    Spurge, Prostrate Spurge

Preparation and Uses: This large and interesting

genus has plants of varied uses. Some of the species are thought to be good in treating rattlesnake bite *(E. albomarginata).* One *(E. hirtula)* is used today in treating asthma and bronchial congestion. Another's juice *(E. marginata)* has been used in branding cattle in Texas; this species is now grown as an ornamental. The cultivated poinsettia *(E. pulcherrina),* so popular at Christmas, is a well known ornamental.

The root of *E. serpyllifolia* is usually prepared by chewing it for several minutes and then mixing it, saliva and all, with cornmeal to make a tasty bread. The leaves may be chewed for pleasure but are usually not swallowed nor mixed into bread dough. It should be noted that quite a number of *Euphorbia* species are poisonous.

Habitat and Distribution: Spurge is generally distributed throughout the West in dry, open ground.

Description: The plant is an annual forming mats up to 3 feet across. The stems are slender, often reddish at the base, are prostrate, and much-branched. The leaves are opposite, smooth, round to oblong, dull green on top and paler beneath, about ¼ inch long, and minutely toothed toward the apex. The stipules are fringed. The flowers are white and clustered in a circle of bracts in the leaf axils.

17. *Mentzelia albicaulis* (1) (Loasa Family)
    Whitestem Mentzelia, Stickleaf

Preparation and Uses: A nutritious meal may be ground from the parched seeds.

Habitat and Distribution: The plant is found in arid, sandy soil from Wyoming to Washington, south to New Mexico, Arizona, and California.

Description: The shiny, silvery stems of Mentzelia are usually freely branched, covered with very fine short hairs, and are often long and sinuous. The leaves are sessile, and rough to the touch. The lower leaves are narrow, and broader toward the tips than toward the base. The upper leaves are linear. The yellow flowers have 5 petals. The tuberculate seeds are in a capsule.

18. *Reseda lutea* (1) (Mignonette Family)
Yellow Mignonette

   Preparation and Uses: The young plants are good in salads.
   Habitat and Distribution: This native of Europe has become established on roadsides, hills, and waste places in California and Colorado. It should be looked for elsewhere in the West.
   Description: The plant is a more or less hairy herb with both erect and downward bending stems. The deeply lobed leaves are oblong to linear, with gently wavy margins. The greenish-yellow flowers are borne in narrow racemes.

19. *Cleome serrulata* and related species (6)
(Caper Family)
Rocky Mountain Bee Plant, Bee Plant, Stinkweed, Spiderflower

   Preparation and Uses: The boiled leaves and flowers may be eaten as greens.
   For use as dye, the plants are collected in quantity and boiled down until a thick, fluid residue is produced. This is drained off and allowed to dry and harden into cakes. When black dye or paint is desired, a piece of the cake is soaked in hot water.
   Habitat and Distribution: Rocky Mountain Bee Plant is found in sagebrush areas and in the more arid forests throughout the West.
   Description: The stems of these plants are mostly tall and branched. The leaves are simple or pal-

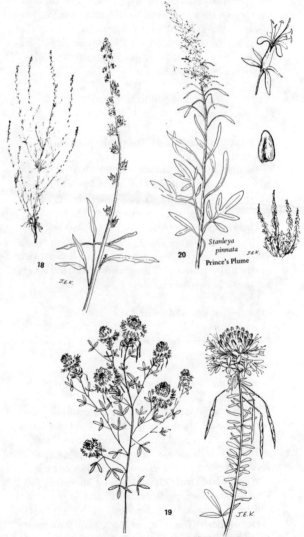

Stanleya pinnata
Prince's Plume

18

19

20

mately compound with 3 to 5 leaflets. Sepals number 4. Petals number 4 and bear a distinct claw. Stamens number 6 and are inserted in a receptacle above the petals. The flowers are yellow, golden, purplish, rose, or white.

20. *Stanleya* species (5) (Mustard Family)
Prince's Plume, Desert Plume

Preparation and Uses: The tender stems and leaves have a cabbage-like taste and may be prepared in the same way as cabbage. Some of the species are quite bitter at first, but boiling in several waters removes the astringency. The seeds may be parched and ground, and eaten as mush or used in other ways.

Habitat and Distribution: Prince's Plume is found in dry ground throughout the West.

Description: The various species range from annuals to perennials, the latter frequently being somewhat woody near the base. They may be smooth or hairy; the stems may be branched or simple. Basal leaves, sometimes forming a rosette, rise from the roots or extreme base of the plant. The stem leaves may or may not be petioled. The white to yellow flowers are in a long raceme.

21. *Caulanthus crassicaulis* (1) (Mustard Family)
Squaw Cabbage, Wild Cabbage

Preparation and Uses: The plant is best eaten as a green when young and it needs to be cooked. The leaves and young stems are placed in boiling water for a few minutes, removed, washed in cold water and squeezed. This process should be repeated 5 to 6 times to remove the bitter taste, after which they may be used as boiled cabbage. The seeds may be eaten parched or ground into flour.

Habitat and Distribution: Squaw Cabbage is

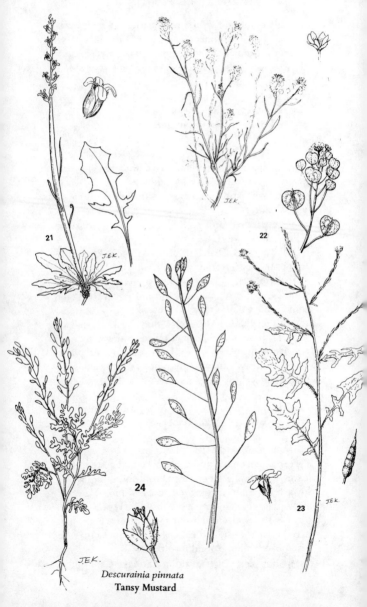

21

22

24

23

Descurainia pinnata
Tansy Mustard

found in open woodlands, particularly pinon-juniper, in California, Arizona, Nevada, southern Idaho, Colorado and Wyoming.

Description: The plant is a short-lived herbaceous perennial with unbranched, hairless, whitened stems from 10 to 40 inches tall. The stems are stout and hollow. The basal leaves are in a rosette, are hairless, and are sometimes whitened with a waxy substance; they vary from entire and oblanceolate to deeply cleft, the terminal lobe being larger than the others. The leaves on the upper stems are entire. The sepals are purplish to brown, linear, channeled, and curved outward. The flowers are on short stalks.

22. *Lepidium fremontii* and related species (2)
   (Mustard Family)
   Pepper Grass

Preparation and Uses: The seeds mixed with vinegar and a little salt make an excellent dressing for meat. The seeds may be used directly as flavoring in salads, soups and stews, and are nutritious. The young shoots of the plants are good in salad.

Habitat and Distribution: The various species are widely spread throughout the West in moist to dry habitats.

Description: The Pepper Grasses are annual or perennial herbs, some being slightly hairy. The flowers are very small, and bear yellow or white petals. Sometimes the petals are entirely lacking. The stamens are often 4 in number, but sometimes number only 2. The leaves are entire to compound, the latter being composed of 2 or 3 leaflets. The leaves sometimes clasp, or even entirely surround, the stem.

23. *Sisymbrium officinale* (1) (Mustard Family)
   Hedge Mustard, Flax Weed

Preparation and Uses: The seeds may be parched and ground into a nutritious flour. The young plants make a good potherb.

Habitat and Distribution: This plant is an abundant weed in fields and waste places throughout the West.

Description: Hedge Mustard is an annual, stiffly erect herb with a few widely diverging branches, and hairy near the base. The hairy leaves form a basal rosette. The yellow flowers are borne in long, narrow, racemes. The small oval seeds are dark brown.

24. *Descurainia* species (5) (Mustard Family)
    Tansy-Mustard

Preparation and Uses: All of the species are edible, although some are better than others. They may be eaten as greens and the seeds may be parched, ground, and eaten as mush or used in other ways. The Mexicans use the seeds in poultices for wounds.

One species, *D. pinnata,* is reported to be poisonous to livestock, but only when eaten in large quantities over a long period of time. It causes partial or complete blindness, accompanied by an inability to use the tongue or to swallow; literally a paralyzed tongue.

Habitat and Distribution: The various species are found mainly in dry, open ground throughout the West.

Description: Tansy-Mustard is an annual plant, sometimes glandular, stellate-pubescent, with tall, leafy, simple or sparingly branched stems. The leaves are deeply pinnately cleft, but the clefts do not extend to the midrib. The leaves may also be once to thrice pinnate, with small segments. The racemes are terminal, becoming elongated. The small flowers are whitish or yellow. The seeds are

small, many, and in 1 or 2 rows in each cell of the
2-celled capsule.

25. *Brassica nigra* and related species (9) (Mustard
    Family)
    Mustard

   Preparation and Uses: Most of the species make
quite palatable greens with the seeds removed, and
all are edible. *B. nigra* and *B. juncea* are useful as
skin stimulants; the seeds may be ground or crushed to a flour and applied as a mustard plaster.

   The cultivated cabbage, cauliflower, mustard,
turnip, Brussels sprouts, broccoli, rutabaga, kale,
and others are included in this genus.

   Many of the species, including the cultivated ones,
have caused poisoning in livestock. It is therefore
assumed that great quantities of any of them would
prove toxic to humans. In the case of the mus-
tards, however, it seems to be the seeds that cause
the trouble.

   Habitat and Distribution: The plants are found
in open fields, meadows, and waste ground throughout the West.

   Description: Mustard plants are annual to perennial, erect, branched herbs. The basal leaves are pinnately divided into narrow lobes that do not reach
the midvein. The stem leaves are quite variable:
some, especially the lower ones, may be lobed; in
some species the stem leaves are toothed; in some
they may be almost entire. The large, showy, yellow flowers are in elongated racemes.

26. *Barbarea verna* and *vulgaris* (2) (Mustard Family)
    Winter Cress, Yellow Rocket, Scurvy Grass

   Preparation and Uses: The young stems and
leaves may be eaten raw in salads although they are

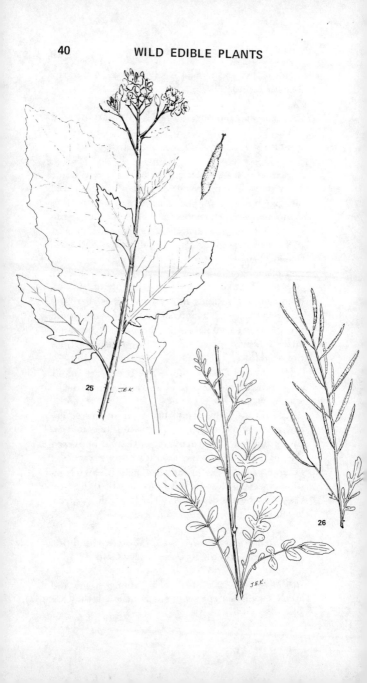

too bitter to suit some people. The young stems
and leaves do make good potherbs, however, when
boiled in 2 waters which remove most of the bitter
taste. It is probable, but not known for sure, that all
of the species in this genus are edible. *B. verna,*
Scurvy Grass, is cultivated in the southeastern
United States and sold on the market.

Habitat and Distribution: Winter Cress is found
in rich, moist ground, but is rather sparingly distributed throughout the West.

Description: These hardy herbs have a basal rosette of leaves that last through the winter, often
growing vigorously during warm spells. The stems
are noticably angled. The leaves are pinnately divided into narrow lobes that do not reach the midvein. The lobes of the basal leaves, however, are
divided to the midvein. The yellow flowers are
borne in racemes.

27. *Nasturtium officinale (Rorippa nasturtium-*
    aquatica) and related species (13)
    (Mustard Family)
    Water Cress

Preparation and Uses: Water Cress is well known
as an excellent salad plant but it is also good cooked as a potherb. For several thousand years the
plant has been eaten by people all over the world.
During Roman times in Italy and other Mediterranean areas it was considered good for deranged
minds.

Pliny (23-79 A.D.) lists over 40 medicinal uses
for Water Cress, including the knowledge that the
smell of burned Water Cress was supposed to drive
away serpents and neutralize the venom of scor-
pions.

To other ancients Water Cress was something to
be avoided. According to the Greek physician
Dioscorides (40-70 A.D.), the seed of these plants

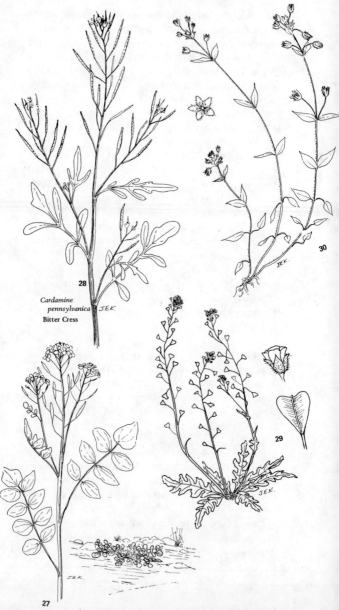

*Cardamine
pennsylvanica* J.E.K.
Bitter Cress

28

30

29

27

was bad for the stomach, harmed the spleen, and killed the unborn child, although they would expel worms. He also felt that the seeds of Water Cress were a good aphrodisiac, but Pliny said that they had the opposite effect. In any case, many people of that time, and before, ate Water Cress.

Habitat and Distribution: Water Cress is found in springs and slow streams throughout the West.

Description: The plant is a floating, erect or prostrate, aquatic herb forming masses along the edge of a slow stream, and with anchored roots. White roots often show at nodes along the floating stems. The small white flowers are in terminal racemes. The smooth leaves are pinnate.

28. *Cardamine* species (15) (Mustard Family)
    Bitter Cress, Spring Cress

Preparation and Uses: These plants are good raw in salads or better cooked in various ways, depending on the cook's imagination and ability. Some are better than others, *C. pensylvanica* being one of the best.

Habitat and Distribution: The various species are found in moist places, sometimes with their roots in moving water, throughout the West.

Description: The Bitter Cresses are annual or perennial herbs, mostly hairless, although some have soft, spreading hairs. The stems bear entire, lobed, rather long petioled, broadly oval leaves. The white or purple flowers are in racemes or rather flattopped clusters.

29. *Capsella bursa-pastoris* (1) (Mustard Family)
    Shepherd's Purse

Preparation and Uses: The seeds may be parched and eaten, or ground into flour.

Habitat and Distribution: Shepherd's Purse is

found in waste places throughout the West.

Description: The plant is an annual with tufted basal leaves in a rosette. The leaves may be entire or toothed. The flowers are very small, white or pink, and occur in elongate racemes.

30. *Stellaria media* (1) (Pink Family)
Common Chickweed, Chickweed, Starwort

Preparation and Uses: When boiled, Chickweed resembles spinach in flavor. The young, growing tips are best since the plant becomes stringy with maturity. The plant has been widely used in Europe, where it is native.

Habitat and Distribution: Chickweed is a common weed in shady areas, in waste ground, about fields, etc., throughout the West.

Description: Chickweed is an annual with weak and reclining stems that are tufted with hair. The opposite, oval, entire leaves are rather sharp pointed. The lower leaves are petioled; the upper ones are not. The small, white flowers are borne in terminal leafy clusters.

31. *Silene cucubalus* and *acaulis* (2) (Pink Family)
Bladder Campion, Catchfly, Campion, Maidens Tears, and Mossy Campion

Preparation and Uses: The young shoots, not over 2 inches in length, make a good potherb. The entire plant above ground of *S. acaulis* may be boiled until tender and eaten.

Habitat and Distribution: The two species are, between them, found throughout the West. *S. cucubalus* is found in waste areas, fields, and roadsides from 7000 to 9000 feet. *S. acaulis* is a high altitude plant, found from 10,000 to 12,500 feet.

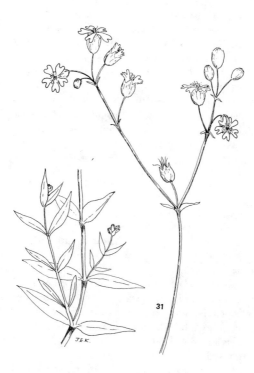

31

Description: Bladder Campion is a hardy perennial rising from thick, spreading rhizomes. The stems are usually hairless and covered with a delicate white, powdery substance. The leaves are narrowly oval-shaped. The pale green to purplish calyx is thin walled and inflated, hence the common name of Bladder Campion. The flowers are white; the seeds brown.

Moss Campion is a densely tufted, matted pink or purple flowered plant that is hairless to finely hairy. The crowded, sessile, leaves are linear and have a finely toothed margin bearing a fringe of hairs. The flowers are solitary at the ends of the branches.

32. *Portulaca oleracea* and related species (6)
(Purslane Family)
Purslane

Preparation and Uses: Although the young leaves and branches are best, the entire plant above ground may be cooked and seasoned like spinach, or used in salad. The boiled mass may be chopped and combined with bread and beaten eggs to make a superb dish. An excellent meatloaf may be made by adding ground meat, venison making it especially flavorful. The young shoots also make a good pickle. Bread and mush may be made from the ground seeds.

The species listed above is reported to be a native of India, from whence it spread, first to southeast Asia, then to Europe, and finally to the New World, where it has become well established throughout. It is an excellent food plant that has been in recorded use for several thousand years. Europeans use it extensively, as did the American pioneers. In view of this it is surprising that today this superb food plant is considered an obnoxious weed in gardens.

Claytonia lanceolata

Spring Beauty

34

Habitat and Distribution: Purslane is widely distributed throughout the West in cultivated and waste ground.

Description: The Purslanes are fleshy herbs with mostly alternate leaves. The flowers are in close terminal clusters, usually opening only in sunshine, and have 2 sepals and 5 petals, which are pale yellow in *P. oleracea*. Occasionally there are more than 5 petals. The sepal tube coheres on the ovary; the petals are borne on the calyx.

33. *Lewisia rediviva* (1) (Purslane Family)
     Bitterroot

Preparation and Uses: Although it is probable that all the species have edible roots, *L. rediviva* is the only one well known to have been used extensively. The nutritious root is quite variable in its bitter qualities: some of them will be so bitter as to render them unpalatable when raw, while others will be quite palatable. In any case, cooking removes most or all of the bitterness and improves the flavor. The root should be boiled to a jelly-like consistency which will frequently be of a pink color. The bitterness can be greatly reduced by peeling the root before boiling, to expose the white, starchy, and somewhat mucilaginous core. In early spring the bitter peel will slip off by vigorously rubbing the root between the hands.

The plant is the state flower of Montana and was introduced by the Indians to Captain Meriwether Lewis of the Lewis and Clark expedition, which used it as food. It was collected and carried back to Washington, D.C., where the noted British botanist, Frederick Pursh, named it in honor of Lewis.

Habitat and Distribution: Bitterroot is found in dry, open, and often stony ground in Montana, British Columbia, south to Colorado, Utah, and northern California.

Description: The plant is low and somewhat fleshy with thick roots. The conspicuous, white to pink flower often comes out after the basal leaves have withered, so that the plant appears to be leaf-less. The leaves appear almost as soon as the snow melts and are strap-shaped. The root is carrot-shaped.

34. *Claytonia* species (4) (Purslane Family)
Springbeauty

Preparation and Uses: The small bulbs may be eaten raw, boiled, or roasted. They will improve the flavor of any stew.

Habitat and Distribution: Springbeauty is found in varied habitats in mountainous country throughout the West.

Description: These plants are small, smooth perennials with the base of the stem thickened into a large edible bulb. There is 1 pair of opposite, narrow, lanceolate, stem leaves. The flowers are few, conspicuous, pale pink and in loose racemes. Sepals number 2. Petals and stamens number 5. The style is 3-cleft.

35. *Montia perfoliata (Claytonia perfoliata)* and
related species (17) (Purslane Family)
Miners Lettuce, Indian Lettuce, Springbeauty

Preparation and Uses: The stems and leaves may be eaten raw or boiled like spinach. An excellent salad can be made of canned tuna mixed with Miners Lettuce leaves, and seasoned with a dressing of olive oil, salt, pepper, vinegar, and spices to suit. The roots are edible raw and are rather pleasing when boiled, having the flavor of chestnuts.

This plant was a favorite of the vegetable-starved 49'ers in early California. This is one of the relatively few native plants that has been introduced into Europe where it is cultivated and goes under the name of Winter Purslane. It has also been introduced on some Caribbean Islands such as Cuba.

Habitat and Distribution: Miner's Lettuce is found in moist ground throughout the West.

Description: The plants are annual *(M. perfoliata* is an annual) or perennial herbs. The somewhat fleshy, basal leaves may be opposite or alternate. The pink or white flowers are often in simple racemes. In *M. perfoliata* the stem appears to pierce the leaves. These plants exist in some taxonomic confusion, but, in general, those with tubers or corms are classified as *Claytonia,* while those without such rootstocks are *Montia.*

36. *Mollugo verticillata* (1) (Carpetweed Family)
    Indian Chickweed, Carpetweed

    Preparation and Uses: The plant may be used as a potherb.

    Habitat and Distribution: A native of tropical America, Indian Chickweed may be found in sandy, moist areas throughout the West.

    Description: The plant is a matlike, hairless, annual with unequal, spatula-shaped leaves arranged 5 to 6 in a whorl. The flowers have no petals, but have 5 sepals that are white on the inside.

37. *Opuntia polyacantha, basilaris* and related species
    (41) (Cactus Family)
    Prickly Pear Cactus, Indian Fig, Tuna, Beavertail

    Preparation and Uses: The fruits and new joints are peeled and the pulp may be eaten raw, or boiled and then fried or stewed. The pulp can be sun or fire dried for future use.

    The fruits of the larger species are especially sweet and flavorful and were extensively used by the Indians and early pioneers. All species bear

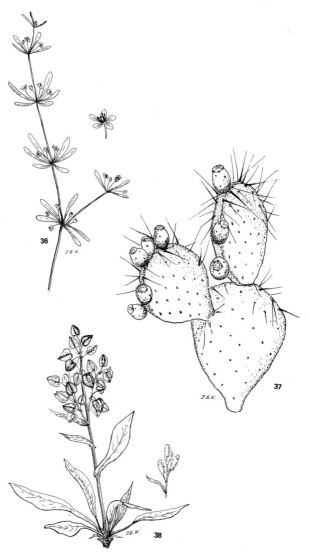

36

37

38

edible fruits but some are so small or become dry
so quickly that they are of little value.

An excellent syrup can be made from the
larger species by boiling down the peeled fruits and
straining out the seeds. The syrup makes an excellent base for tasty jelly and candy.

The seeds may be eaten in soups or dried and
ground into flour.

It is interesting to note that no cactus is native
to the Old World, but they have been heavily introduced from the New World. Some, such as *O.
Fiscus-indica,* a large-growing cactus from Mexico,
were once much cultivated for their excellent fruits.
O. Fiscus-indica (Indian Fig, Tuna) was introduced
into the Southwest by Spanish missionaries and
cultivated. They used the fruits in the manner
described above, and sometimes further reduced
the syrup to make a dark red to black paste known
as *Queso de Tuna.* These plants are still used in
Mexico, and not a few people eat them in California.
Many Mexican people yet today cut the young
joints into strips and boil them as a potherb, or pickle them.

Indians and early pioneers of the Southwest
used the split, fleshy pads, after soaking in water, of
these cacti for binding wounds and bruises. A bitter
juice may be crushed from the fleshy pads to assuage
one's thirst, if water is not available. In Mexico the
pads are boiled and crushed, the sticky juice being
added to whitewash or mortar to make it stick
more securely.

Habitat and Distribution: These cacti are
found in desert areas throughout the West.

Description: There are two basic types of
Opuntia. The ones with flattened, fleshy joints
are referred to above; the other type has dry,
woody, cylindrical joints and are referred to as
Cholla. These produce nothing edible. The species
are extremely variable according to environment

and they hybridize freely, so that positive identification is not at all necessary and the flat-jointed *Opuntia* as a whole are quite distinctive and easy to recognize. The flat, broad, spiny, fleshy joints are enough to identify them.

38. *Rumex hymenosepalus, crispus,* and related species (31) (Buckwheat Family)
Wild Rhubarb, Canaigre, Dock, Sorrel

Preparation and Uses: These are plants that can, like garden rhubarb *(Rheum rhaponticum)* be poisonous if not used properly. However, there are no human deaths attributed to the use of *Rumex* species, while there are to common rhubarb. Garden rhubarb leaf stems owe their pleasant tart flavor largely to malic acid, while the leaf blade is tart because of the presence of oxalic and citric acid. No deaths have resulted from eating the stems (petioles) of garden rhubarb, but death has resulted from eating the leaf blades, since oxalic acid is toxic.

All of the species of *Rumex* bear edible leaves and leaf stems, but some have less acid than others, a fact easily discerned by tasting their tartness. Those that are particularly tart or bitter should be boiled two or three times in fresh water, which will remove most of the acid and yet leave a pleasant flavor. The last boiling should be done with as little water as possible so that the leaves and leaf stalks will not be so watery as to be unpleasant when eaten. A number of the species need the leaves and petioles boiled only once, according to personal taste.

R. hymenosepalus produces leaves that are quite good boiled or roasted. The petioles of the leaves of *R. hymenosepalus* are an excellent substitute for rhubarb in pies. The root of this species is extremely high in tannin and efforts are underway to cultivate the plant commercially. The

Navaho Indians formerly extracted a dye from the roots, and the Hopi and Papago used them for treating colds.

Rumex poisoning has been recorded only in livestock after rather large quantities were eaten.

Habitat and Distribution: The various species are found throughout the West in many habitats, from dry, sandy soil to moist ground, mainly in the open.

Description: These plants are mostly perennial herbs, but some are annuals. Their grooved stems are simple or branched, mainly with large basal leaves. The small, numerous, mostly greenish flowers are crowded in whorled, panicled racemes. The fruit is a 3-angled, veiny nutlet.

39. *Oxyria digyna* (1) (Buckwheat Family)
    Mountain Sorrel, Scurvy Grass, Alpine Sorrel

Preparation and Uses: The leaves and stems have a pleasant sour taste when eaten raw in salads, and are also good when boiled. Various Indian tribes, expecially some of those in Canada and Alaska, ferment Mountain Sorrel slightly as a sort of saurkraut. Others store it for winter use. The plants are high in vitamin C and were used in early times to prevent and cure scurvy.

Habitat and Distribution: Mountain Sorrel is found at high altitudes in mountains throughout the West.

Description: The plant is a succulent herb with long-stalked, round, or kidney-shaped leaves rising from the stem close to the root. The numerous, small, greenish to crimson flowers are usually crowded and whorled in panicled racemes.

40. *Polygonum* species (45) (Buckwheat Family)
    Knotweed, Smartweed, Knotgrass, American Bistort, Sacca, Sachaline

*Polygonum
bistortoides*
Knotweed
40

Preparation and Uses: Many of the Knot-
weeds such as *P. aviculare,* have seeds that may be
used whole or ground into flour. Others have peppery leaves which make good seasonings. Still
others, such as *P. bistortoides* and *P. viviparum,*
have starchy roots that are edible raw or boiled,
but are best when roasted. Some species, such as
P. cuspidatum and *P. sachalinense,* have foliage
that, when young, makes good salads or potherbs,
and they also have edible roots. *P. sachalinense*
(Sacca or Sachaline) was introduced from Asia
around 1870 or earlier and has spread rapidly. It
is widely cultivated in Asia, some in Europe, and
even a little in the United States as a garden vegetable.

The genus deserves experimentation since none
of the species are listed as poisonous. The sap of
many species is quite acid, however, and no doubt
could produce intestinal disturbances if eaten raw
in large quantities.

Habitat and Distribution: The various species
are found in many habitats: moist, dry, saline,
rocky, sunny, shady, etc., throughout the West.

Description: These plants are annual or perennial herbs, or sometimes shrubs rising from thick
roots. The jointed stems are often swollen at the
nodes. The alternate leaves are usually simple and
entire. The usually thin, dry, stipules are united
in a cylindrical sheath. The small flowers are in
spikes, racemes, or scattered in the leaf axils. The
fruits are either three-angled or lens-shaped.

41. *Chenopodium fremontii* and related species
    (35) (Goosefoot Family)
    Goosefoot, Pigweed

Preparation and Uses: All of the species are more
or less edible, although the one listed above is the
best. The leaves may be cooked as greens. In late

summer the small black seeds can be eaten raw; they are best when salted, mixed with corn meal, and made into mush or cakes.

The roots of *C. californicum* make excellent soap when used fresh or dried and ground to a powder. *C. ambrosioides* yields oil of chenopodium, which is a good cure for intestinal worms.

Large quantities of the plants could prove toxic due to the oil mentioned above. They probably should only be eaten in normal quantities.

Habitat and Distribution: Pigweed is widely distributed throughout the West in the more arid regions, and is found in many habitats.

Description: The plants are herbaceous annuals or perennials, usually mealy, sometimes glandular. The leaves are alternate, and entire to lobed. The flowers are green, perfect, axillary or forming spikes or panicles, and are in heads. They are fleshy with 2-5 lobes and 2-5 stamens.

42. *Cycloloma atriplicifolium* (1) (Goosefoot Family)
Winged Pigweed

Preparation and Uses: The ground seeds may be boiled as mush or made into cakes.

Habitat and Distribution: The plant is found in fields and groves in dry, sandy ground from Indiana to Manitoba, south to Texas, New Mexico, Colorado, Arizona and southern California. Not found in the Northwest.

Description: Winged Pigweed is an annual herb with diffusely branched stems 4-20 inches tall. The leaves are alternate, petioled, oblong, and have a wavy, toothed margin. The flowers are in a broad panicle, the perianth being 5-lobed. Stamens number 5. The seeds are black.

Atriplex canescens
Saltbush

43. *Monolepis nuttalliana* (1) (Goosefoot Family)
Patata, Povertyweed

Preparation and Uses: The plant above ground may be eaten as a potherb. The seeds may also be used.

Habitat and Distribution: Patata is found in moist, often saline, ground throughout the West.

Description: The somewhat fleshy stem is pale green and branched at the base, the branches stout and ascending, although somewhat prostrate. The leaves are narrowly triangular, sometimes with a few teeth, and lobed near the base. The often reddish flowers are in dense clusters.

44. *Atriplex* species (41) (Goosefoot Family)
Saltbush, Shadscale

Preparation and Uses: The seeds are quite nutritious and may be ground into meal, mixed with water and drunk as a refreshing beverage, or mixed with some other meal and used as flour. The leaves and young shoots may be used as greens; they have a distinct salty taste and are excellent when boiled with meat. The ashes of *A. canescens* make a good substitute for baking powder.

Saltbush is one of those plants which can absorb selenium, if it is present in the soil. Selenium is well known to be toxic to livestock and presumably would be toxic to humans were they to ingest sufficient quantities. This situation has not been reported, however, and, in any case, plants growing in selenium free soil are safe. (see Glossary on selenium)

Habitat and Distribution: Saltbush is widely scattered throughout the West in arid, alkaline, or saline soil.

Description: The plants are perennial or annual, herbaceous or shrubby, covered with minute scales or granules giving them a grayish or whitish, mealy appearance. The leaves are commonly alternate but are also found opposite, and entire to a toothed, deeply wavy margin. The sexes may be found on separate plants or they may not. The flowers are small, green, and in axillary clusters or spikes.

45. *Kochia scoparia* (1) (Goosefoot Family)
Summer Cypress

Preparation and Uses: The tips of the young shoots may be eaten as a potherb. The seeds may be eaten raw or cooked, or ground into meal and made into bread.
The plant is a native of Eurasia and was introduced into the United States as an ornamental. In Japan, China, and other Asian countries it is cultivated for its edible seeds.
Habitat and Distribution: Summer Cypress has escaped gardens and may be found growing in open, waste areas nearly throughout the West.
Description: Summer Cypress is an erect, branched, densely leafy, hairless to sparsely hairy annual, often heavily tinged with red. The leaves are lanceolate to linear in form. The small flowers are borne in axillary clusters. The midrib of each sepal becomes thickened with age.

46. *Salicornia* species (4) (Goosefoot Family)
Glasswort, Samphire, Pickleweed

Preparation and Uses: These succulent, salty-tasting plants make a good salad. The young shoots and branches make a good pickle when first boiled and then put in any pickling mix.
Habitat and Distribution: California contains all four species in saline or alkaline, marshy ground *S. europaea (S. rubra)* is found throughout the West in salty or alkaline ground, except, apparently, for Arizona.

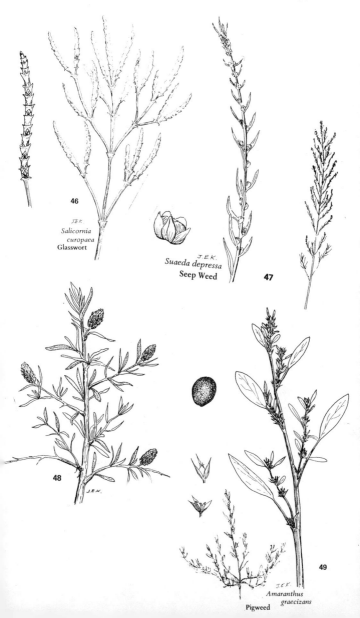

46
J.E.K.
*Salicornia
europaea*
Glasswort

Suaeda depressa
Seep Weed

J.E.K.

47

48
J.E.K.

*Amaranthus
graecizans*
Pigweed

49

Description: These plants are fleshy, hairless, herbaceous annuals with leafless, jointed stems bearing opposite branches. The leaves are opposite and are quite reduced and scalelike. The flowers are borne in fleshy, cylindrical, spikes with the flowers sunk in groups of 3 to 7 in cavities on opposite sides of the joints.

47. *Suaeda* species (7) (Goosefoot Family)
    Seep Weed, Desert Blite

Preparation and Uses: The seeds may be eaten raw or parched. The young plants are edible as greens and have a salty flavor. They are good when cooked with cactus fruits. A black dye can be made by soaking masses of the stems and leaves for many hours in water.

Habitat and Distribution: The Seep Weeds are found in alkaline and saline soil throughout the West.

Description: The plants are succulent, perennial or annual herbs with more or less fleshy, alternate, entire, rounded to spatula-like (in cross-section) leaves. The flowers are in cylindrical, fleshy spikes, and occur in clusters at the nodes, each flower with a minute bractlet.

48. *Sarcobatus vermiculatus* (1) (Goosefoot Family)
    Greasewood

Preparation and Uses: The tender young growing twigs may be washed, cut into short pieces, boiled several hours until tender, seasoned with salt and butter, and eaten.

Habitat and Distribution: Greasewood is a common shrub of alkaline soil throughout the more arid areas of the West.

Description: Greasewood is a highly branched,

somewhat spiny shrub. The younger branches are grayish - to yellowish - white. The fleshy, sessile leaves are flattened above and rounded underneath.

49. *Amaranthus* species (18) (Amaranth Family)
Amaranth, Pigweed

Preparation and Uses: The young leaves of any of the species may be used as greens but should be boiled without delay after gathering to keep the fine asparagus-like flavor. As greens, these leaves are much superior to spinach. In late summer, the small black seeds mature and may be eaten raw or mixed with corn meal and salt, added to ground meat and steamed as meat balls or meat patties.

The seeds of *A. cruentus* were used by the Hopi Indians of northern Arizona to color corn bread pink and for ceremonial functions.

Since some Pigweed can accumulate dangerous levels of nitrates and thus cause nitrate poisoning, they should not be collected for eating in large quantities in cultivated areas where nitrate fertilizers may be spread on the ground. Normal amounts eaten at a single meal have no danger whatever.

Habitat and Distribution: The various species are found scattered throughout the West in moist to dry ground in many different habitats.

Description: The plants are herbaceous annuals with petioled, pinnately veined alternate leaves. The flowers are small, mostly unisexual and very often have a bract and two bractlets at the base. The flowers have 2 to 5 segments which are distinct and 2 to 5 stamens.

50. *Glaux maritima* (1) (Primrose Family)
Sea Milkwort

Preparation and Uses: The young leaves and stems are good when pickled.

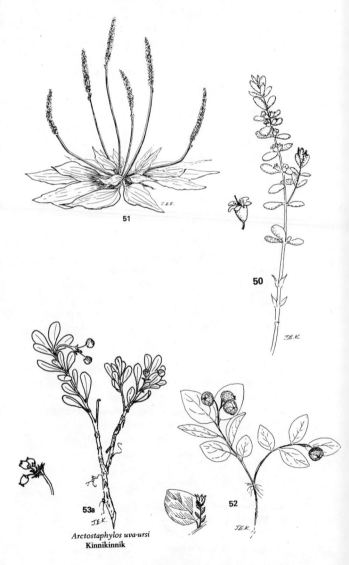

Arctostaphylos uva-ursi
Kinnikinnik

Habitat and Distribution: Sea Milkwort is found in saline and subsaline soil throughout the West, except, apparently, for Arizona.

Description: The plant is a low growing, fleshy, perennial rising with slender stems from rootstocks. The opposite, entire, fleshy, leaves are sessile, linear to oblong, and have tips varying from roundish to sharp pointed. The small white, reddish, or lavender flowers are borne in the axils.

51. *Plantago major* and related species
    (22) (Plantain Family)
    Plantain, Indian Wheat

Preparation and Uses: The young plants may be used as a potherb or in salads. As they age the leaves of some species become quite fibrous. The seeds may be eaten parched or ground into meal. The seeds have a mucilaginous coat and make a good laxative when soaked in water and eaten raw.

Habitat and Distribution: The various species are found in moist ground throughout the West.

Description: The Plantains are annual or perennial herbs with basal, longitudinally ribbed leaves. The small inconspicuous flowers are in dense spikes on leafless stems.

52. *Gaultheria humifusa* (1) (Heath Family)
    Western Wintergreen

Preparation and Uses: The small red fruit is edible raw or cooked, as are the leaves. The young, tender leaves are especially suited for use as greens. Both fruit and leaves have a wintergreen flavor.

Habitat and Distribution: Western Wintergreen is found in open ground and woods from Alberta to British Columbia and southward to California and Colorado.

Description: This plant is a low evergreen shrub

with alternate leaves and small pink or white flowers. The flowers are borne in the leaf axils on branches that are 1 to 4 inches long. The half inch long leaves are rounded to oval. The fruit is red.

53. *Arctostaphylos* species (43) (Heath Family) Manzanita

Preparation and Uses: The acid berries may be eaten right from the bush although they are hard to digest in quantity when raw. They make good pies, cobblers, and excellent jelly. They may be eaten in quantity when stewed, or dried and ground into meal and cooked as mush.

A good beverage is made as follows: The berries are scalded for a few minutes or until the seeds are soft, and then they are crushed to a pulp. To a quart of this is added a quart of water. The mixture is allowed to settle for an hour or more and is then strained. When cool, this "cider" is spicy, acid, and ready to drink without sugar. A number of Californians still concoct this drink; some even make wine from the berries.

The seeds of the berries may be removed and ground into flour.

A. uva-ursi (Kinnikinick, Indian Tobacco) provides leaves and bark that, when dried, make a pleasant smoke. Its berries may be used as above. A decoction of the leaves of this species is sometimes used today by Arizona old-timers to treat urinary disorders. Drugs are today commercially extracted from the leaves and used as astringents and diuretics. The leaves were once used for tannin production and still are in Russia.

A decoction of the leaves of *A. pungens* has been used in Arizona to cure stomach trouble.

Habitat and Distribution: The plants in this genus are found throughout the West in dry, but not desert ground. Kinnikinick probably has the greatest range, extending from Alaska south to California and east to the Rockies in mountainous country.

Description: These are woody, evergreen plants, varying from low prostrate and spreading shrubs to small trees with many crooked branches usually bearing thin, deep red to brown bark which can be seen peeling off in layers on the larger branches and main trunk. The leaves are simple, alternate, entire to finely saw-toothed, sessile or petioled, and tough and leathery. The flowers are small and in terminal clusters; the fruit is berry like.

54. *Vaccinium* species (13) (Heath Family)
Huckleberry, Blueberry, Whortleberry, Bilberry

Preparation and Uses: These sweet berries were widely used by Indian groups and early western settlers. They are still extensively gathered from the wild, and some species are today grown commercially. The berries are delicious raw, make excellent pies and jellies, are good in pancakes and muffins, and dry and keep well.

Habitat and Distribution: Huckleberries are found in the more moist habitats of the mountains throughout the West.

Description: These plants vary widely in form from slender and almost vining to large, stout shrubs, depending on the species. The simple, alternate leaves may be either evergreen or deciduous, again depending on the species. The 4 to 5 petals are united so that they often resemble an urn. The berries are blue-black, blue, or red.

55. *Moneses uniflora* (1) (Wintergreen Family)
Woodnymph

Preparation and Uses: The seeds, along with their capsule, are edible raw, roasted, parched, ground, etc.

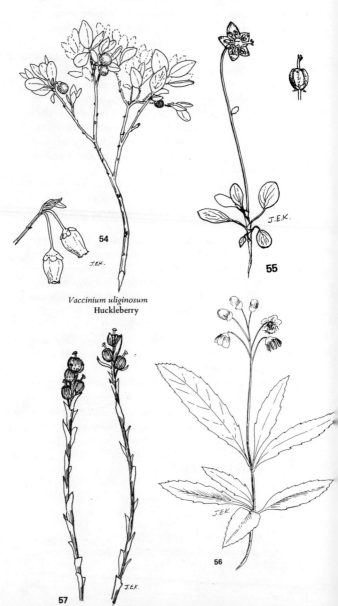

Vaccinium uliginosum
Huckleberry

Habitat and Distribution: The plant is rather rare, but widely distributed in deep, moist, cool woods throughout the West.

Description: Woodnymph is an herbaceous perennial rising from slender rootstock. The leaves are basal, in 2's or 3's, rounded, veiny, thin, and with petioles almost as long as the leaf itself. The minute seeds are numerous.

56. *Chimaphila umbellata* (1) (Wintergreen Family)
Prince's Pine, Pipsissewa

Preparation and Uses: The roots and leaves may be boiled, and the liquid allowed to cool to produce a refreshing drink. The pleasingly flavored leaves may be nibbled raw. The leaves are used as an astringent in the manufacture of some modern medicines. The plant is also an ingredient in root-beer.

Habitat and Distribution: Prince's Pine is found on moist to dry, shrubby to wooded slopes, and along streamsides throughout the West.

Description: The plant is a low, evergreen, somewhat shrubby perennial with branching stems rising from underground rootstocks. The thick, short-petioled, toothed, oblanceolate leaves are yellow-green on the underneath side, and borne in whorls of 3 to 8. The pink flowers are borne on stalks 2½ to 3¼ inches long.

57. *Monotropa hypopithys* and *uniflora*
(2) (Wintergreen Family)
Pinesap, Indian Pipe

Preparation and Uses: Pinesap is edible raw or cooked.

Habitat and Distribution: The plant is found in rich soil throughout the West.

Description: These plants are parasitic or saprophytic, perennial herbs. The clustered stems are simple. The many leaves are scale-like. The entire plant is pinkish to white. The roots form a dense, matted clump. The solitary, nodding flowers are relatively large, bear 2 to 4 sepals, and 4 to 6 petals.

58. *Frasera speciosa* (1) (Gentian Family)
    Elkweed, Green Gentian,
    Deer Tongue, Deer's Ear

Preparation and Uses: The fleshy root of this plant may be eaten raw, roasted, or boiled, and is good when mixed with other potherbs or raw greens.

Elkweed is a member of the Gentian family, many members of which are used medicinally the world over. *Frasera carolinensis* has been used as a cathartic and emetic, but *F. speciosa* does not have such an effect when eaten in normal quantities.

Habitat and Distribution: The plant is found mostly above 5000 feet in moist to medium dry, open areas throughout the West.

Description: First year growth is a cluster of large, long, strongly veined leaves. The next year shows the development of a very stout flower stem rising from a large taproot, and bearing many greenish-white flowers with purple spots. The flowers are on stalks rising from upper leaf axils on the main stem. Both mature and first-year growth will be found growing in the same area.

59. *Asclepias speciosa* (1) (Milkweed Family)
    Showy Milkweed, Milkweed

Preparation and Uses: The flowers may be eaten raw or boiled; the buds, young shoots and young leaves are good as greens or boiled in soup with meat. The seeds and the inner wall of the pod may be eaten raw or cooked. An excellent brown sugar can be boiled down from the flowers. *A. tuberosa*

58

59

J.E.K.

J.E.K.

has roots which may be cooked and eaten. The plants contain latex.

A number of *Asclepias* species, including the one listed above, are known to be poisonous in varying degrees. Normal quantities of *A. speciosa,* used in the manner outlined above, are safe, however.

The Hopi Indians believe that *A. subverticillata* increases the flow of milk in women. All of the milkweeds of this genus contain asclepain, a good meat tenderizer. The United States Department of Agriculture once considered the possibility of using the seed hairs of certain species in place of kapok in filling life rafts.

Habitat and Distribution: Showy Milkweed is widely distributed throughout the West in dry, open ground.

Description: The plant is stout, erect, herbaceous and entirely covered with satiny, short hairs. The flower arrangement is densely woolly. The leaves are rather heart-shaped to ovate or oblong. The flowers are purplish and are borne in dense, many flowered umbels.

60. *Hydrophyllum occidentale* and related species
    (4) (Waterleaf Family)
    Waterleaf

Preparation and Uses: The young shoots are excellent in salad, or they and the roots may be cooked and eaten.

Habitat and Distribution: Waterleaf is found in moist, rich, often shaded soil in mountains throughout the West.

Description: The plants are perennial herbs with horizontal rootstocks, fleshy or tuberous roots, and soft, succulent stems and foliage. The leaves are alternate or mainly basal and pinnately parted and divided. The flowers are greenish to white to violet-blue and more or less densely clustered.

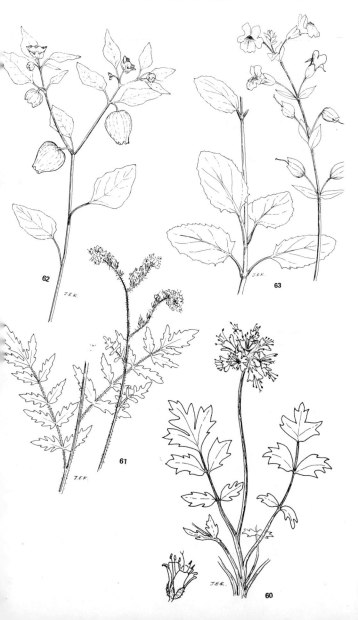

61. *Phacelia ramosissima* (1) (Waterleaf Family)
    Scorpionweed

    Preparation and Uses: The plant may be used as
    cooked greens.
    Habitat and Distribution: Scorpionweed is found
    among shrubs and in rocky places in Washington,
    Idaho, Oregon, California, Nevada, and Arizona.
    Description: This is a perennial plant rising
    from a rather woody base, usually with several
    branching, hairy, stems 20 to 40 inches long. The
    white to bluish flowers are borne in a few rather
    dense, short panicles.

62. *Physalis ixocarpa, longifolia,* and related
    species (18) (Nightshade Family)
    Tomatillo, Ground Cherry, Husk
    Tomato, Strawberry Tomato

    Preparation and Uses: The excellent berries may
    be eaten raw or cooked, but taste best when fully
    ripe. Since they frequently fall to the ground be-
    fore ripe, it is well to gather them and let them
    ripen in the husk where they will keep for weeks.
    In some species the ripening berry will burst the
    husk. Good preserves and pies may be made from
    them. The boiled berries may be crushed with raw
    onions, chili and coriander seeds to make a tasty
    dish. Some species are occasionally commercially
    cultivated for their berries. *P. alkekengi* is fre-
    quently grown as an ornamental.
    The unripe fruit of some species are considered
    poisonous when eaten in sufficient quantity. Bit-
    terness, sourness, or strong flavor indicates unripe
    fruit. Let them ripen until soft and sweet and
    they are safe to eat in quantity.
    Habitat and Distribution: The Ground Cherries
    are found in moist to medium dry, open ground
    throughout the West.

Description: The plants are annual or perennial herbs with alternate, entire to coarsely toothed leaves. The flowers are usually solitary in the axils but occasionally are found in clusters of 2 to 5. The calyx is 5-lobed, becoming greatly enlarged and inflated in fruit. Within this is the berry. The flowers are rather obscurely 5-lobed and vary in color from yellowish to white to purple, depending on the species.

63. *Mimulus guttatus* (1) (Figwort Family)
Yellow Monkey-flower, Monkey-flower
Wild Lettuce

Preparation and Uses: The plant may be eaten raw in salads and has a slightly bitter flavor.
Habitat and Distribution: Yellow Monkey-flower is common in moist wet ground throughout the West.
Description: Monkey-flower is an erect-stemmed plant with petioled, hairless to slightly hairy, roundish to oval, unevenly toothed, lower leaves. The broadly oval, toothed, upper leaves are without petioles. The two-lipped, yellow flower has purple to brown dots in its throat.

64. *Veronica americana, anagallis-aquatica, beccabunga, and comosa*
(4) (Figwort Family)
Speedwell, Brooklime, American Brooklime, Water Speedwell

Preparation and Uses: These plants were once widely used as a preventive of scurvy. The leaves and stems may be eaten in salads or used as pot-herbs.
Habitat and Distribution: The Speedwells are found in moist to wet ground throughout the West.
Description: These herbaceous plants bear opposite leaves. The rather wheel-shaped, white to

blue flowers are 4-lobed, the upper lobe being broad. Stamens number 2; the stigma is entire.

65. *Castilleja linariaefolia* and related species
    (60) (Figwort Family)
    Indian Paint Brush, Painted Cup

> **Preparation and Uses:** Many, perhaps all, of the species have flowers that may be eaten raw, but the one listed above is the best. It is the state flower of Wyoming.
>
> When selenium is present in the soil many of the species have the ability to absorb it. Care should be taken, therefore, to eat only normal quantities.
>
> **Habitat and Distribution:** The plants are found throughout the West, mostly in dry, open ground, but a few occur in moist habitats.
>
> **Description:** Indian Paint Brush is a conspicuous herb with alternate leaves and red flowers borne in dense terminal spikes. The flowers are subtended by bright red or crimson leafy bracts. The corolla is very irregular with the upper lip much larger than the lower, arched, and colored greenish-yellow tinged with scarlet.

66. *Orobanche fasciculata* and related species
    (11) (Broom Rape Family)
    Broom Rape, Ghost Plant

> **Preparation and Uses:** The entire plant, including roots, is edible raw, but is best when roasted in the hot ashes of a campfire.
>
> **Habitat and Distribution:** Broom Rape is found on plains, hills, and slopes throughout the West.
>
> **Description:** All of the species are parasitic on the roots of other plants. They are not green, even though they are flowering plants, but vary from yellow or yellowish brown to white. Their alternate leaves are reduced to scales. The irregular

flowers have a 2-lipped corolla, 4 stamens, and 1 pistil. The many very small seeds are enclosed in a capsule.

67. *Verbena hastata* (1) (Vervain Family)
Blue Verbena, Vervain, Blue Vervain

Preparation and Uses: The seeds may be gathered, roasted, and ground into a slightly bitter flour. A little leaching will remove the bitter quality. California Indians, however, rarely bothered to leach the flour.

Habitat and Distribution: Blue Verbena is found in moist places throughout the West.

Description: The plant is an erect, perennial herb growing from 1½ to 4 feet high, and is covered with short hairs. The opposite leaves are lanceolate to somewhat oblong, and are evenly to unevenly toothed. The purplish-blue flowers are clustered at the end of an erect, slender stalk. The seeds are tiny nutlets, less than 2 mm. long.

68. *Marrubium vulgare* (1) (Mint Family)
Horehound

Preparation and Uses: The dried plant becomes a good, nutritious tonic when made into a bitter tea or broth. In large doses it becomes a laxative. Today the use of horehound is limited almost entirely to the production of horehound candy, often used to ease sore throats or cough. Horehound was once used extensively in domestic medicines for colds, dyspepsia, and in expelling worms.

Habitat and Distribution: Horehound is found in dry, open ground, especially waste places, throughout the West.

Description: The erect, clustered, stems branch from the base and are densely covered, to the point of being woolly, with white or greenish hairs.

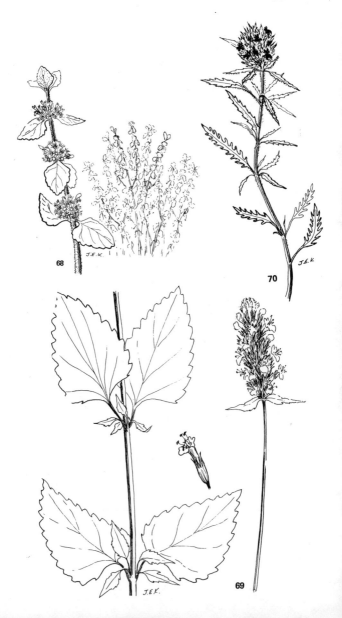

The leaves are roundish to oval, dentate or scal-
loped, wrinkled, with fine white hairs on top, and
woolly ones on the underneath side. The flowers
are white to purplish.

69. *Agastache urticifolia* (1) (Mint Family)
Giant Hyssop, Horsemint

Preparation and Uses: The seeds may be eaten
raw or cooked.

Habitat and Distribution: The plant is found in
moist, open soil mostly in coniferous forest areas
throughout the West except for Arizona and New
Mexico.

Description: Giant Hyssop is a tall perennial
herb with oval, toothed, petioled leaves on branching stems. The rose to violet flowers are borne in
dense, unstalked whorls. The nutlet-like seeds are
dull brown.

70. *Moldavica parviflora (Dracocephalum parviflorum)*
(1) (Mint Family)
Dragon Head, American Dragon Head

Preparation and Uses: The Havasupai Indians of
northern Arizona are reported to make a nutritious
flour from the seeds, as did early western pioneers.

Habitat and Distribution: Dragon Head is found
in dry, often rocky, open ground and woods
throughout the West except for California.

Description: This herbaceous plant grows from
6 to 30 inches high with more or less hairy stems.
The coarsely serrate leaves are lanceolate to oblong,
with the lower ones sometimes oval in shape. The
pale blue to light rose flowers are whorled in a terminal head with bristle-tipped bracts.

71. *Prunella vulgaris* (1) (Mint Family)
Common Self-Heal

Preparation and Uses: A refreshing beverage can be made from this mint by chopping the leaves and soaking them in cold water, or by drying them and finely powdering them in cold water. Common Self-Heal was once considered to be of medicinal value.

Habitat and Distribution: This is a very common mint usually found in moist, shaded ground throughout the cooler parts of the West.

Description: The plant has a typical square mint stem which may be solitary or in clusters, 4 to 12 inches high with oblong or egg-shaped leaves. The lower leaves are petioled, the upper ones sessile. Flowers occur in dense terminal spikes with bracts, and are purple, violet, or blue in color.

72. *Glecoma hederacea* (1) (Mint Family)
Ground Ivy, Gill-over-the-Ground

Preparation and Uses: The leaves may be dried and used for tea. Ground Ivy has been known to fatally poison horses that ate it in large amounts. No instance of human sickness has been recorded, however, and the plant has long been used for tea in its native Europe.

Habitat and Distribution: Ground Ivy is common in shaded, moist, ground throughout most of the West.

Description: The plant is a creeping, perennial herb forming a distinctive ground cover. The square, jointed stems bear pairs of roundish leaves plus roots at each joint or node. The blue to bluish-purple flowers are borne in the leaf axils.

73. *Lamium amplexicaule* (1) (Mint Family)
Henbit, Dead Nettle

Preparation and Uses: Henbit may be boiled alone, or with other ingredients, and eaten.

71

72

74

73

Habitat and Description: Henbit is a weed of fields, and coastal ground, throughout the West.

Description: The plant is a low herb, sparsely hairy, with the stem branching from the base; some stems bending down. The lower leaves are roundish to oval to heart-shaped, have rounded teeth on the margin, and long petioles. The upper leaves are similar to the lower, but have no petioles, and clasp the stalk. The purplish to red flowers occur in axillary and terminal clusters.

74. *Stachys palustris* (1) (Mint Family)
Betony, Hedge Nettle, Swamp Hedge Nettle

Preparation and Uses: The tubers of this plant, produced in autumn, may be eaten raw, roasted, or boiled. Although all of the species of this genus producing tubers are reported edible this cannot be confirmed. Careful experimentation with the other western species would be in order.

A wash for sores and wounds may be concocted by making an infusion of the fresh leaves of any of the various species. The leaves may be soaked in water for a few minutes and used as a poultice.

Various species of this genus have long been cultivated in Asia, including Japan, for their tubers, where they go by the name of Chinese Artichoke.

Habitat and Distribution: Betony is found in moist, open soil throughout the West.

Description: The plant has slender, simple or few-branched, hairy stems rising 2 to 3 feet high. The pale rose flowers have red veins, and are in whorls on terminal spikes. The oblong to lanceolate leaves are usually rounded at the base.

75. *Salvia columbariae* and related species
(32) (Mint Family)
Chia, Sage

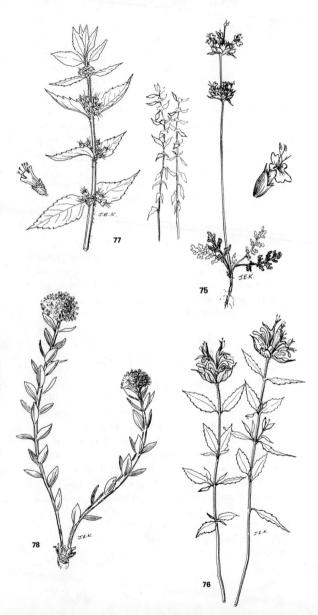

Preparation and Uses: The seeds may be eaten raw, or parched and ground into flour. A good, although mucilaginous, beverage may be made by mixing ¼ cup of the flour in cold water and stirring vigorously. A spoonful of the whole seeds may be soaked in a glass of water for 15 to 20 minutes to make a flavorful beverage, especially when a little sugar and lemon juice are added.

One species, *S. officinalis,* is the garden sage that provides the well known flavoring.

Habitat and Distribution: These plants are found in prairies, plains, fields, and along roadsides throughout the West.

Description: These sages are strongly aromatic annual or perennial herbs or shrubs. The opposite entire to coarsely toothed leaves are sometimes mostly basal. The flowers are usually whorled in interrupted spikes, racemes, or panicles. The seeds are smooth nutlets.

76. *Monarda menthaefolia* (1) (Mint Family)
Beebalm, Horsemint

Preparation and Uses: The entire plant above ground may be used as a potherb, or dried for future use. Beebalm makes excellent flavoring when cooked with other food, and good tea may be steeped from the leaves. Thymol, an antiseptic drug, is obtained from some of the species.

Habitat and Distribution: Beebalm is found in moist to medium dry soil, mostly in pine forests, in Arizona and New Mexico, entering valleys and plains north to Alberta. It is found in pine forest and open valleys in Colorado and Wyoming.

Description: Beebalm is a perennial herb with square, upright, usually unbranched stems that are finely hairy above and hairless below. The leaves are somewhat oval, serrate, with the underneath surface finely haired, the upper surface hairy or hairless, and arranged oppositely on the stem. The rose to purple flowers are in roundish heads.

77. *Mentha arvensis* (1) (Mint Family)
    Mint, Wild Mint, Field Mint

Preparation and Uses: An excellent tea may be made by steeping the fresh or dried leaves in hot water for a few minutes. Members of the mint family are widely used in commerce. Menthol is derived from a cultivated variety of the native mint listed above. Spearmint is derived from *M. spicata* and peppermint from *M. piperita,* both Old World species that have become widely naturalized in the United States. Other mint extracts are used as flavoring agents, in perfume, and in medicines. All three species listed here make good tea, and can also be used for making jelly.

Habitat and Distribution: Mint is widely distributed throughout the West in wet ground.

Description: This is an aromatic herb strongly smelling of mint. The usually branched stems are square with sharply toothed leaves. The flowers are white, pink, or even violet in color, with the upper lobe larger than the other three.

78. *Sedum rosea* and related species
    (12) (Stonecrop Family)
    Stonecrop, Orpin

Preparation and Uses: Stonecrop makes a good salad plant or potherb. When using the plant for salad the best flavor is obtained from the young stems and leaves. Some stonecrops are better tasting than others. *S. acre,* for example, is too acid to be very palatable.

Habitat and Distribution: The various stonecrops are found on ledges, banks, cliffs, and other moist, rocky places throughout the West.

Description: The stonecrops are herbs, although some species are almost shrubby. They are usually hairless, and bear mostly alternate leaves, often small, that overlap each other. Sometimes the leaves are in basal or terminal rosettes. Often the leaves are fleshy. The yellow, white, or red flowers are borne in cymes.

79. *Heuchera* species (28) (Saxifrage Family)
Alum-root

Preparation and Uses: Occasionally campers or hikers contract diarrhea from drinking alkali water or other causes. The roots of these plants, eaten raw, form an effective cure.

Habitat and Distribution: Alum-root is found in woods and on slopes, in mountains and foothills throughout the West.

Description: These plants are perennial herbs with a leafless (or leaves reduced to bracts), flower-bearing stem arising from a somewhat woody, scaly, thickened base. The leaves are nearly all basal, long-petioled, roundish and flat, with indented bases.

80. *Ribes* species (24) (Saxifrage Family)
Currants and Gooseberries

Preparation and Uses: The berries of all species may be eaten, although some are better tasting than others. They may be eaten raw or cooked, and are good when dried in the sun. They make excellent pies and jellies. Various western Indians used the berries in making pemmican, *(refer to glossary)*. The berries of *R. cereum* were used by the Hopi Indians to relieve stomach-ache.

The various *Ribes* species are the alternate host to the White Pine Blister Rust, the most deadly

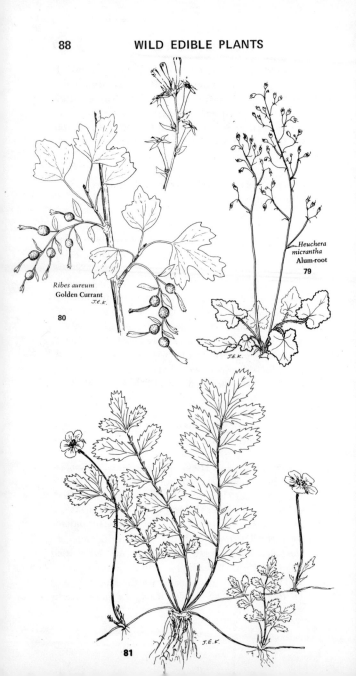

*Heuchera
micrantha*
Alum-root
79

Ribes aureum
Golden Currant
J.E.K.
80

81

fungus disease of Western White Pine, and other 5-needle pines, although harmless to animals. One method of control is to totally eliminate all *Ribes* plants from an infected area.

Habitat and Distribution: The various species are found in many different habitats throughout the West, although they all require a fair amount of moisture. In mountain areas they are found in moist soil in shaded or open land. In desert areas they may be found around springs, in gullies, or at the base of cliffs where there might be underground water close to the surface.

Description: In general, currants are without spines while gooseberries are quite prickly. They are shrubs with alternate, palmately veined leaves. The flowers are usually in racemes, or solitary, perfect and regular, on 1 to 2-leaved axillary stems. The 5-lobed calyx tube is completely fused with the ovary, and the petals are inserted on the tube. The sepals and petals number 5, rarely 4; the petals are usually shorter than the sepals. The stamens are alternate with the petals. The fruit forms a berry.

81. *Potentilla anserina* (1) (Rose Family)
Silverweed, Goose Tansy, Goosegrass,
Cinquefoil, Five-finger

Preparation and Uses: The roots are good boiled or roasted, after which they taste something like parsnips.

Habitat and Distribution: Silverweed is found in moist to wet, often saline or alkaline soil throughout the cooler parts of the West.

Description: The plant is a low-growing perennial, spreading by means of runners, with rosettes of leaves that are pinnately divided into numerous leaflets that, in turn, are pinnately veined with toothed margins. The leaves are green and almost hairless on the top side, and white with densely matted, woolly hairs beneath. The yellow flowers are solitary.

82.　*Fragaria* species (8) (Rose Family)
　　Wild Strawberry

Preparation and Use: The berries, though small, are sweet and delicious; many people prefer them to domestic varieties. They may be used in the same way as cultivated strawberries.

Some western Indians prepared tea from the green leaves. A gourmet commercial tea, available on the market, contains some strawberry leaves for added flavor.

Habitat and Distribution: These plants are found in sandy, often moist, ground, in open woods, open fields and hillsides throughout the West. Not found in desert areas.

Description: Strawberries are perennial herbs with the flower stems, runners, and leaves arising from a scaly rootstock. The leaves have 3 leaflets. The flowers are usually white and borne in a small flower cluster. The red fruit is that of a typical strawberry.

83.　*Sanguisorba occidentalis, minor* and related
　　species (5) (Rose Family)
　　Burnet

Preparation and Uses: The young leaves make a good salad plant.

Habitat and Distribution: The various species range from bogs to fields and open sandy ground in Montana, Idaho, Washington, Oregon, California, and Arizona. They should be looked for in the remaining western states.

Description: The plants are leafy, mostly perennial herbs, with leaves that are unequally pinnately

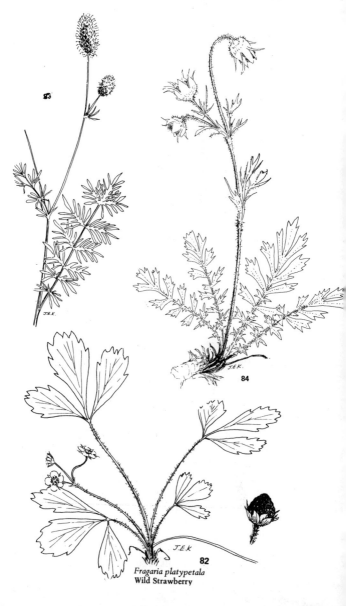

82
Fragaria platypetala
Wild Strawberry

compound and bear toothed leaflets. The small
flowers form dense white to reddish purple or purple spikes or heads at the end of long, naked stalks.

84. *Geum ciliatum* (1) (Rose Family)
Prairie Smoke, Oldman-whiskers, Grandfathers-
beard, Longplumed Avens.

Preparation and Uses: The roots may be boiled
to produce a tea.
Habitat and Distribution: Prairie Smoke is
found on dry to moist, rocky slopes, plains, and
hillsides throughout the West.
Description: The plant is a finely ¦glandular
perennial, covered with soft hairs, and rises from
fairly large rootstocks. The stipuled leaves are
pinnate. The basal leaves are tufted. The rather
large, yellow to purplish-tinged flowers are borne
in a cyme.

85. *Cercocarpus ledifolius* and related species
(7) (Rose Family)
Mountain Mahogany

Preparation and Uses: The scraped bark makes
a flavorful additive to a brew of Mormon tea
(*Ephedra*).   A beautiful red dye may be obtained
from the bark and roots.
Habitat and Distribution: Mountain Mahogany
is found throughout the West on hills and in canyons, often in rocky ground. Mahogany sometimes
covers many acres in almost pure stands.
Description: The plants are evergreen shrubs or
small trees. The leaves are alternate, simple, fas-
cicled, straight veined, and entire or dentate. The
flowers are solitary or in small close clusters, axillary or terminal, inconspicuous, with 5 small, yellowish sepals and no petals. The fruit is cylindric,
spindle-shaped, small, dry, one-seeded, and bears a
terminal elongate silky, feathery or plum-like style.

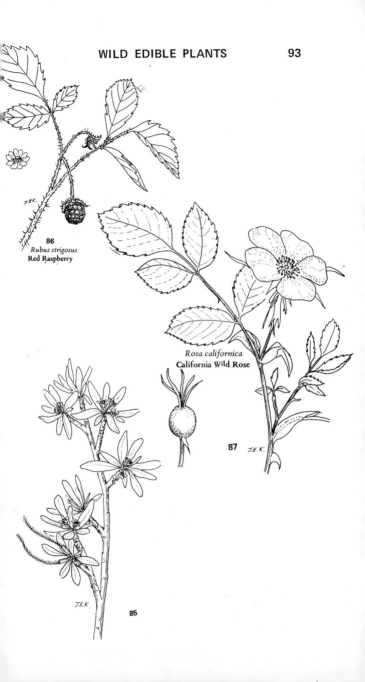

86
Rubus strigosus
Red Raspberry

Rosa californica
California Wild Rose

87

85

86. *Rubus* species (23) (Rose Family)
     Raspberries, Blackberries, Thimble-
     berries, Dewberries, Blackcaps

Preparation and Uses: All of the species produce edible berries which are excellent raw or in jellies and pies.

Habitat and Distribution: These plants are found in mountainous country throughout the West, mostly at the higher altitudes.

Description: *Rubus* species are shrubs, with or without spines, and have alternate, simple and pal- mately lobed leaves, or compound leaves. The stems are flowering, clustered, and usually some- what woody, especially near the base. The fruits form a red, black, purple, bluish or even orange to yellow berry, depending on the species.

87. *Rosa* species (17) (Rose Family)
     Wild Rose

Preparation and Uses: The edible fruits, often called rose hips, can be eaten raw, stewed, candied, or made into preserves. A little sugar improves the flavor. Some species have pulpier fruits than others and are therefore better for use.

The petals of the flowers are pleasant tasting and may be candied or used in salads. The petals of the cultivated *R. gallica* provide us with rose oil, used in making perfume.

The ancients had many uses for the rose, both medicinal and superstitious. It was believed that petals of the flower, along with other items accord- ing to a prescribed formula, prevented a tree from bearing fruit when hung among its branches.

Habitat and Distribution: The Wild Rose is found wherever there is sufficient moisture, and proper climate.

Description: These prickly, shrubby plants are easy to identify as roses. Their alternate leaves are pinnate. The mostly rose-pink, fragrant flowers are solitary, and are borne in panicles. The petals and sepals number 5.

88. *Prunus virginiana* and related species (16)
     (Rose Family)
     Common Chokecherry, Western Chokecherry,
     Wild Cherry, Stone-fruit

Preparation and Uses: The fruit ripens in July and August and is quite sour when raw, although edible. When cooked, the sourness disappears. Sugar much improves the flavor. Chokecherries make excellent jelly.

Many species in this genus are known to have toxic amounts of cyanide in their leaves and are thus a threat to livestock. The pits of the cherries (including cultivated cherries) also have dangerous levels of cyanide. A number of human deaths, mostly children, have been recorded from eating cherries without extracting the pits. Cyanide is volatile so cooking will free the pits of the poison. Such common commercial products as apricots, almonds, and peaches are also *Prunus* species that have pits that contain cyanide. We do eat, of course, the nuts to be found within the pits of commercial almonds. These have some cyanide but it is not in dangerous concentrations. Bitter almonds, on the other hand, do contain dangerous amounts of cyanide.

The pits of one or even several of any of these species are not, as a rule, dangerous, but they become so when eaten in quantity.

Habitat and Distribution: Chokecherries are found in well watered places throughout the West, especially mountainous areas.

Description: Cherries and plums are both species

88

J.E.K.

89
Sorbus scopulina
Mountain Ash

of *Prunus* and differences are slight. In general, the plums are larger, have fleshier fruit and more flattened pits than do cherries. These plants are trees or shrubs with simple, usually toothed leaves. The flowers appear early in spring and have 5 sepals and petals with many stamens. The fruits of the Western Chokecherry are dark red to black.

89. *Sorbus* species (7) (Rose Family)
    Mountain Ash

   Preparation and Uses: The berries may be eaten raw, cooked, or dried. Unripe berries are too bitter to be eaten. When thoroughly ripe, and after some frost-mellowing, they become quite palatable. Early western settlers made them into pies, jams, jellies, and even a bitter-sweet wine.

   The genus is spread around the world in the northern hemisphere and the berries are still used in some areas of Europe and Asia.

   Habitat and Distribution: The various species are found mostly in moist soil in the mountainous areas of the West.

   Description: These plants vary from deciduous shrubs to trees, depending on the species. They have alternate, pinnate leaves. The white flowers are borne in terminal, rather flattopped clusters. Sepals and petals number 5.

90. *Amelanchier species* (9) (Rose Family)
    Service Berry, Sarvice Berry

   Preparation and Uses: All of the members of this genus produce edible berries, some in greater quantity than others. The berries ripen in late spring and on through the summer, depending on the elevation, and have a pleasant, often sweet flavor. They may be eaten raw, cooked, or dried.

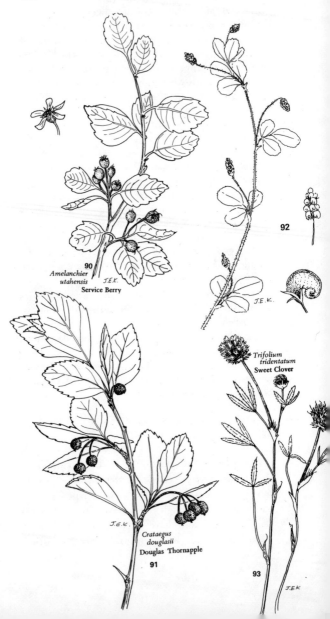

90
Amelanchier
utahensis   J.E.K.
Service Berry

92

Crataegus
douglasii
Douglas Thornapple
91

Trifolium
tridentatum
Sweet Clover

93

Western Indians often dried them and pounded them together in loaves which weighed from 10 to 15 pounds. The loaves will remain sweet and may be eaten after softening a piece in water, or after placing pieces of the loaves in soups or stews. The fresh berries are excellent in pancakes. A number of western people today prepare the berries in jam, jelly, and wine. There is one commercial jelly of this berry made in Montana.

One eastern species is sometimes cultivated for the berries.

Habitat and Distribution: The various species are widely distributed throughout the West in moist to rather dry ground, in clearings, and along streams and lake sides. The best berries are found on those bushes growing in moist habitats.

Description: Service Berry plants are large shrubs or small trees with simple leaves. The leaves are petioled and may be serrate, dentate, or nearly entire. The flowers are fairly large, white, and in groups or sometimes solitary. There is 1 compound pistil with 2-5 styles. The stamens are numerous. The ripe fruit is bluish and fleshy.

91. *Crataegus species* (5) (Rose Family)
Hawthorn, Haw, Thorn Plum,
Black Hawthorn

Preparation and Uses: All species produce edible berries but some produce fleshier fruit than others. The berries are edible raw and make good jams and jellies. Western Indians ate the berries fresh, dried, or mixed into pemmican.

Habitat and Distribution: Hawthorns are found in woods and thickets, and along streams throughout the West.

Description: These plants are shrubs to small trees and have long, sharp thorns. The simple, petioled, toothed to lobed, alternate leaves are strongly veined. The urn to cup-shaped, white or pink, 5 petaled flowers are borne in flattopped clusters. The berries are purple-black, red, or yellow in color.

92. *Medicago lupulina* (1) (**Pea Family**)
    Black Medick, Nonesuch

Preparation and Uses: The seeds may be parched and eaten, or ground into flour. *M. sativa* is the cultivated alfalfa of commerce.

Habitat and Distribution: The plant is an obnoxious, introduced weed, widely distributed through the West in waste places.

Description: Black Medick is a many-branched, rather prostrate herb with more or less hairy stems. The leaves are divided into roundish leaflets, the ones above bearing small, irregular teeth on the margin. The light yellow flowers are in short, dense, spikes.

93. *Trifolium species* (63) (**Pea Family**)
    Sweet Clover, Red Clover, Clover,
    Trefoil

Preparation and Uses: The plants can be eaten raw, but sparingly as they are hard to digest and can cause bloat. However, due to the high protein content they are quite nutritious and can be eaten in quantity if cooked, or soaked for several hours in strong salt water.

The seeds and dried flowers may also be used for food. A flavorful tea may be made by steeping the dried flowers for a few minutes in hot water. The tea is said to be a good tonic.

Habitat and Distribution: The many species of Clover are found in varied habitats throughout the West, even in rather dry areas.

Description: Almost everyone can recognize the various clovers as herbaceous plants with palmate leaves divided into 3 leaflets. The flower heads vary in color from white, yellow, pink, rose, to purple.

94. *Glycyrrhiza lepidota* (1) (**Pea Family**)
Licorice

Preparation and Uses: The sweet roots have a pleasant flavor when eaten or chewed raw, or added to other foods as flavoring. Our American species is in no way inferior to the Old World cultivated licorice, *G. glabra,* which contains considerable quantities of flavorings, sugar, and compounds used in medicine, candy, root beer, chewing tobacco, and fire extinguisher chemicals.

Habitat and Distribution: Licorice is usually found in patches in moist meadows and valleys throughout the West.

Description: The plant is an erect, branching, perennial herb, 1-3 feet tall, with thick rootstocks. The pinnate leaves have 11-19 leaflets. The yellowish-white flowers are in dense racemes rising from the leaf axils. The seed pods are dotted with hooked spines.

95. *Hedysarum occidentale, sulphurescens,* and *alpinum (boreale)*
(3) (**Pea Family**)
Sweetvetch, Licorice Root, Sweetbroom, Western Hedysarum

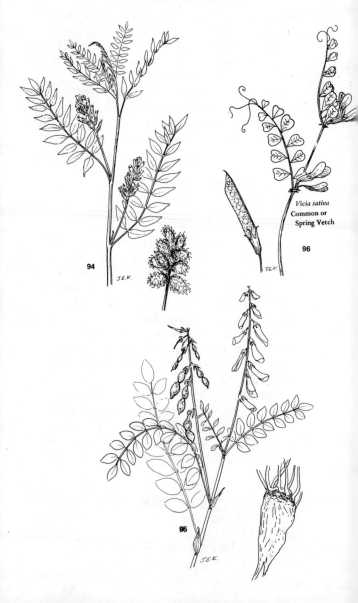

Vicia sativa
**Common or
Spring Vetch**

96

94

95

Preparation and Uses: The 3 species listed above have nourishing, edible roots, tasting faintly like carrots when cooked. The raw roots of *H. occidentale* have a sweet licorice taste. These plants were well known to Indians and early trappers. There is some controversy about a few of the species. For example, *H. Mackenzii* is listed as quite edible by one 19th century writer, and poisonous by another. Since none of the species of this genus are officially listed as poisonous it is probable that all are edible.

Habitat and Distribution: Sweetvetch is found in dry ground throughout the West, except for California. In Oregon it is reported only from the Wallowa Mountains.

Description: The plants are perennial, clustered, upright herbs with numerous, smooth stems growing from a thick taproot. The keel of the flower is nearly straight, and is longer than the wings. The flowers are bright, reddish-purple to white to bright yellow, depending on the species.

96. *Vicia species* (19) **(Pea Family)**
    Vetch, Wild Pea

Preparation and Uses: The young stems and tender young seeds are good when boiled or baked. One species, *V. faba,* the Greek Bean, has been cultivated in the Old World for literally thousands of years. It has many medicinal uses as well as its basic value for food.

Habitat and Distribution: The various species are widely established in moist to dry, open ground throughout the West.

Description: The plants are strongly reminiscent of garden peas, in whose family they belong. They

are mostly vinelike herbs with pinnate leaves
usually bearing climbing tendrils. The yellow to
white to purple flowers are borne in axillary racemes or on solitary-flowered, axillary peduncles.
The typical pea pod is flattened and contains
within it small peas.

97. *Quercus gambelii* and related species (36)
     (Oak Family) Gambel's Oak,
     Rocky Mountain White Oak

   Preparation and Uses: All of the oaks produce
edible acorns, but in general, the white oaks are
superior to the black oaks in producing sweet
acorns. Gambel's oak is listed above as being preferred because its acorns may be eaten as they
come from the tree. Other oaks are better after
some of the tannin has been leached out of the
acorns; in some cases this is an absolute necessity.
Leaching may be done in several ways. Probably
the best procedure is to grind the thoroughly
dried acorns into flour and leach out the tannin
with water. This may be done by putting the meal
in a bag and immersing it in a stream for a few
days, kneading the bag every four or five hours
during the day. Another way is to pour hot or cold
water over the meal after it has been placed in a
firmly woven basket, or any container that will
allow the passage of water but not of the meal.
   The Indians of California's Central Valley used
acorns as a staple food and had other methods of
leaching, varying from tribe to tribe. Some would
merely bury the whole acorn in swampy ground for
six to twelve months, after which the blackened
acorns were ready to eat whole.
   Hot water leaches out the tannin faster than
cold water, although it is often thought that this is

97

98 *Salix lutea*
Yellow Willow

99

untrue because the Indians used cold water much more often than hot water. The reason is simply that it was difficult for the Indian to produce hot water in the quantity necessary for leaching.

Once leaching is accomplished, the flour or meal may be used in soups, breads, or other ways.

Habitat and Distribution: Oak trees are found in dry to moist ground in many different habitats throughout the West; they are so ubiquitous that it is practically impossible to classify them in a given habitat.

Description: They are distinctive deciduous or evergreen, hardwood shrubs to large trees, usually with the characteristic oak leaf. However, people unfamiliar with all the varieties of oaks often fail to recognize the live oaks as being in this genus. Probably the best way to identify an oak is by the presence of the acorn, known to almost everyone.

98. *Salix species* (31) (Willow Family)
Willow

Preparation and Uses: The bitter inner bark of any of the willows may be eaten raw as an emergency food. It is more palatable when dried and ground into flour.

Habitat and Distribution: Willows are found in moist to wet ground throughout the West, from sea level to above timberline.

Description: Willows are common, well-known shrubs or trees, with very narrow leaves, the trees sometimes being confused with the narrow-leaved cottonwood. This is of no importance, since the inner bark of the cottonwoods *(Populus* species) may be used in the same way as the willow. The willow twigs are usually slender and smooth-barked,

and bear simple, narrow, pinnately veined leaves.
The flowers are in catkins.

99. *Celtis douglasii* and *C. pallida*
(2) (Elm Family)
Hackberry and Desert Hackberry

Preparation and Uses: The small orange, red, or
yellow fruit is edible raw and is sweetish. It may
be dried and ground, pit and all, into flour. The
Papago Indians still consider the fruit a good food
source.

Habitat and Distribution: Hackberry is found
along streams or dry canyon slopes east of the
Oregon Cascades north to Washington and Idaho,
and south to California, Nevada, Utah, New Mexico,
Arizona, and Colorado.

Description: The plants are trees or shrubs. The
leaves are simple, alternate, unequal at the base
and very rough on the upper surface. The flowers
are perfect or unisexual, axillary, and solitary or in
small racemes. The fruit is yellow to dull red, or
darker, and has thin flesh and a hard-shelled pit.

100. *Urtica gracilis* and related species
(6) (Nettle Family)
Slim Nettle, Stinging Nettle, Nettle

Preparation and Uses: When boiled, the young
shoots and leaves make a good spinach substitute.
Rennet may be made by mixing a quart of salt to 3
pints of a strong infusion of nettles. Mature nettles
were rather widely used in early times in Europe as
a source of fiber, the resulting cloth often being
termed more durable than common linen. A yellow dye may be obtained by boiling the roots.

Habitat and Distribution: Nettles are found along streams and in other moist places throughout the West.

Description: The nettles are annual or perennial, mostly erect herbs with stinging hairs. The opposite, coarsely toothed, strongly veined, petioled leaves are oval to oblong in shape. The mostly greenish flowers are clustered in paired heads or racemes.

101. *Humulus americanus* and *lupulus*
(2) (Mulberry Family)
Hops

Preparation and Uses: There is so little difference between our native wild variety *(H. americanus)* and the introduced, cultivated plant from Eurasia *(H. lupulus)* that at one time the native variety was classified as a subspecies of *H. lupulus.*

Such taxonomic arguments need not worry us since both plants may be used in the same way. Hops are grown for their fruits, used in brewing ale and beer to impart the distinctive bitter taste. Less known is the fact that the young shoots make quite an acceptable potherb. They should be tossed into boiling water for 2 or 3 minutes, removed, and then boiled in fresh water until tender, after which they are delicious.

The seeds and pistillate flowers were used by some Indian groups in making bread. In fact, the Apache name for the plant is said to mean "to make bread with it." The pistillate flowers of a closely related European species are used in brewing malt liquors to give them their characteristically bitter flavor.

Habitat and Distribution: The cultivated hops is

an occasional escapee wherever they are grown. The native species is found in moist land and along streams in Wyoming, Utah, Colorado, New Mexico, Idaho, Nevada, California, and Arizona.

Description: The plant is a perennial, twining vine with opposite, palmately lobed leaves. The sexes are separate: staminate flowers occurring in panicled, loose racemes with a 5-parted flower and 5 stamens; pistillate flowers occurring in 2's in a large conelike spike, the hop, which is used in brewing.

102. *Cannabis sativa* (1) (Mulberry Family)
Hemp, Marijuana

Preparation and Uses: In a number of countries of the world Hemp seeds are widely used as food after being parched. They are often ground into meal, or pressed into cakes.

As is well known, the plant is the source of the drug, marijuana, and also of hashish. In Mexico it is grown for its excellent fiber, hemp.

Although Hemp can be found growing wild in many areas of the West, its cultivation and use as a drug is strictly forbidden by law, and it is grown only by permit, and under rigid control.

The author remembers that, as a boy in a small Colorado town, in the early days of World War II, he was now and then given the unwelcome task of hoeing down the obnoxious and unsightly weeds on the vacant lot next door. The vast majority of these weeds were marijuana plants but no one seemed to care, and furthermore, no one was known to use it.

Habitat and Distribution: Hemp may be found growing in waste ground in many areas of the

104

J.E.K.

103

J.E.K.

J.E.K.

102

West. When discovered, one should report the location to local authorities, who will take steps to eradicate the plants.

Description: Hemp is a stout, erect, coarse, finely hairy, annual herb with opposite, petioled leaves that are 5 to 11 palmately divided. The seeds are gray to brown in color, oval shaped, thick for their length, and hard.

103.   *Epilobium angustifolium* (1)
(Evening Primrose Family) Fireweed

Preparation and Uses: The young shoots and leaves may be boiled like asparagus, or mixed with other raw greens to make salad. The leaves, green or dry, make good tea. The pith of the stems is good in soups. The author knows of a number of people on the Oregon coast who currently use the plant in these ways.

Habitat and Distribution: Fireweed is found in fairly rich, often moist, soil in open woods, thickets, and along streams throughout the West. The plant is often found invading burned-over or cut-over areas, hence the name Fireweed.

In Europe, Fireweed was one of the first plants to appear in the areas devastated by World War II, and brightened the lives of the war-weary residents.

Description: Fireweed is an erect perennial with often reddish, mostly simple stems, 2-6 feet tall. The leaves are alternate, long and lanceolate, nearly entire or minutely toothed, deep green above, and paler beneath. The flowers are magenta or rose-colored and are borne in long terminal racemes.

104. *Oenothera hookeri* and *biennis*
(2) (Evening Primrose Family)
Evening Primrose

Preparation and Uses: The root is good when cooked at the right time of year, usually early spring. At other times it may have a peppery taste. *O. biennis* is a native species that was introduced into Europe and cultivated for its root. Other species in this genus are also known to be edible but the genus is so varied, and hybridizes so readily that it is impossible to say whether or not all of the species are edible.

Habitat and Distribution: Evening Primrose is found in moist ground throughout the West.

Description: The reddish, stout, stems are erect and simple, or branched at the base. The entire or somewhat wavy margined, toothed leaves lie flat on the ground, forming rosettes. The plants are more or less hairy. The flowers of *O. Hookeri* are yellow, turning reddish with age; *O. biennis* flowers are yellow.

105. *Ceanothus* species (57) (Buckthorn Family)
Wild Lilac, Snowbrush, Soapbloom,
Buckbrush

Preparation and Uses: The leaves and flowers make excellent tea when boiled for 5 minutes or so. Some species make better tea than others. An infusion of the bark may be used as a tonic. The fresh flowers of some species make an excellent lather when crushed and rubbed in water, and are said to leave the skin soft and faintly fragrant.

Habitat and Distribution: The Wild Lilac is widely distributed in many habitats throughout the

107

108a

106

*Ceanothus
cuneatus*
Wild Lilac
105

West. It is often found in conjunction with forests or chaparral.

Description: The plants are much branched shrubs with rigid, somewhat spiny branches. The leaves are opposite or alternate, dentate or entire, and heavy veined. The flowers have long clawed, hooded petals, are borne in panicles where the top flowers are the first to develop and later ones arise below. The calyx is connected to the lower part of the ovary. The flowers are white or lilac colored.

106. *Comandra pallida* (1)
(Sandalwood Family)
Bastard Toadflax, False Toadflax

Preparation and Uses: The urn-shaped fruit may be eaten raw, and is best when slightly green, although it is still quite edible when a fully mature brown color.

Habitat and Distribution: The plant is found on mostly dry slopes, often in pine woods, throughout the West.

Description: Bastard Toadflax is an herbaceous root parasite, the hosts being of many kinds of plants. The leaves are alternate and entire. The greenish flowers are borne in few to several-flowered cymes. The fruits are urn-shaped.

107. *Shepherdia argentea* and *canadensis*
(2) (Oleaster Family)
Silver Buffaloberry, Russet Buffaloberry

Preparation and Uses: The berries of the Silver Buffaloberry *(S. argentea)* are pleasantly tart when raw and make good jelly. They may be crushed in water for a good beverage. Travelers across the continent in early days made a sauce of these berries

for their buffalo steaks. The berries dry well and
may be stored in this condition for future use. They
are particularly good when a little sugar is added.

The berries of the Russet Buffaloberry *(S. canadensis)* are insipid and bitter but sugar and cooking
improves their flavor. They were used in the same
way as the silver variety, and they make fine jelly.

Habitat and Distribution: *S. argentea* is found
along streams and in low meadows and stream valleys throughout the West. *S. canadensis* is found
on moist, usually shaded slopes, but toward the
north it is found in open ground; it ranges throughout much of the West except for California.

Description: *S. canadensis* is a thornless shrub
3 to 10 feet tall with brown-scurfy branches when
young. The oval leaves are dark green, smooth on
the top surface, and silvery-scurfy beneath. The
flowers are in clusters at the nodes. The berries
are bright red to pale yellow.

S. argentea forms a shrub to small tree, 6 to 25
feet in height. The thorny branches are silvery-
scurfy when young. The oblong leaves are silvery-
scurfy on both sides and the flowers are at the
nodes. The fruits are scarlet to golden.

108. *Rhus trilobata, glabra,* and *integrifolia*
      (3) (Sumac Family)
      Squaw Bush, Smooth Sumac,
      Lemonade Berry

Preparation and Uses: The berries may be eaten
raw, or soaked in water to which they impart a
lemon-like taste, making a refreshing beverage, especially when a little sugar is added. Lemon pie
may be made from the berries.

It is interesting to note that this genus also contains Poison Sumac *(R. vernix)* of eastern United States, Poison Ivy *(R. toxicodendron)* of the mountainous West, and Poison Oak *(R. diversiloba)* of the far West. All three of these plants can cause serious skin problems when touched; smoke from the burning of any of them can cause blindness.

Habitat and Distribution: These plants are found on slopes, plains, and in canyons throughout the West, wherever there is sufficient moisture.

Description: *R. trilobata* is an erect, bushy, highly branched shrub 3 to 7 feet high. The branches are spreading, often turned down at the tips, and densely covered with fine, short hairs. The hairy leaves are divided into three leaflets. The yellowish flowers are in clustered spikes and develop into reddish, sticky fruits bearing soft, straight, spreading hairs.

109. *Osmorhiza* species (7) (Carrot Family)
 Sweet Cicely, Sweetroot

Preparation and Uses: The roots are strongly anise-flavored and make good seasoning.

Habitat and Distribution: The various species are found throughout the West in wooded areas.

Description: These plants are slender to stout, leafy-stemmed perennials rising from thick, closely-clustered roots. The petioled leaves are in 3's or 3's and 5's. The lobed or toothed leaflets are lanceolate to rounded, and serrate to pinnately divided. The white, purple, or greenish flower cluster is in a loose, compound umbel.

110. *Daucus pusillus* (1) (Carrot Family)
 Carrot, Rattlesnake Weed

Preparation and Uses: This is a relative of the

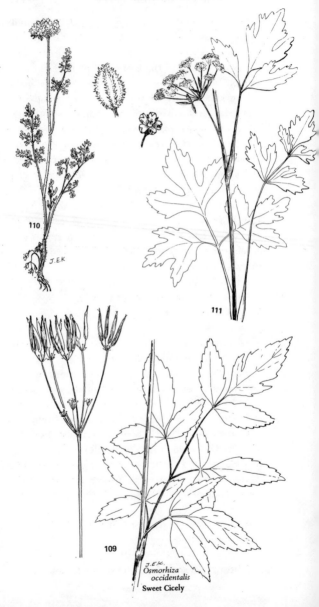

109

*Osmorhiza
occidentalis*

Sweet Cicely

garden carrot and can be prepared in the same way. The Navajo of northern Arizona are reported to still use the plant, eating the roots raw or cooked.

Unfortunately, this plant resembles poison hemlock *(Conium maculatum)*, but the two may readily be distinguished by noting that the carrot has stems and leaves that are distinctly hairy. One should be extremely careful with identification here as *Conium* has been known as an extremely poisonous plant from ancient times. It is believed that an extract of *Conium* was responsible for the death of Socrates, rather than an extract of the water hemlock *(Cicuta)*. Socrates was forced to drink the poison because he had the courage to publicly expound his beliefs, opposing those of his more powerful contemporaries.

Habitat and Distribution: Found in dry, open ground, especially after fire, throughout the West.

Description: A rather bristly annual, 1-2½ feet high, with leaves pinnately divided into small narrow divisions. The plant is few-branched with these bending downward and backward. The flowers are white.

111. *Apium graveolens* (1) (Carrot Family)
Celery

Preparation and Uses: This is common celery, a native of Eurasia, which has escaped cultivation and grows widely throughout North America.

It is interesting to note that this common cultivated plant can absorb dangerous levels of nitrates in the tops. To prevent nitrate poisoning, the tops should either be discarded or eaten in limited quantity.

Habitat and Distribution: The plant is found in

moist, but not alkaline soil throughout the West.

Description: Celery is a stout, smooth perennial with large pinnate leaves bearing few leaflets. The leaves are deeply 3-lobed and mainly circular. The celery stalk is familiar to all.

112. *Perideridia* species (8) (Carrot Family)
Wild Caraway, Yamp, Yampa,
Squawroot, Ipo, Apah

Preparation and Uses: All species of this genus are edible although *P. gairdneri, kelloggii,* and *oregana* are the best. The raw roots have a pleasant, sweet, nutty flavor when eaten raw and resemble carrots when cooked. The small, tuberous roots should be washed and peeled before cooking. They are easily dried and keep well. The dry roots can be ground into an excellent flour. The small seeds may be used for seasoning, or parched and eaten in mush. *P. gairdneri* was widely known and used by Indians and early travelers and settlers in the West.

Habitat and Distribution: Wild Caraway is widely distributed in damp ground throughout the West.

Description: These plants are erect herbs with leafy stems branching from tuberous, clustered roots. The pinnate leaves may be divided into three's. The white flowers are in loose umbels.

113. *Foeniculum vulgare* (1) (Carrot Family)
Fennel, Sweet Fennel

Preparation and Uses: The leaf stalks may be eaten raw or cooked.

Habitat and Distribution: The plant is found in waste ground throughout the West.

Description: Fennel is an erect perennial herb with a leafy stem, and an anise odor. The leaves

Perideridia gairdneri
Wild Caraway

112

115

113

114

are more than once divided into linear divisions. The yellow flowers are in large compound umbels. The sepals are obsolete.

114. *Orogenia fusiformis* and *linearifolia*
(2) (Carrot Family)
Indian Potato, Snowdrops

Preparation and Uses: The roots of these plants are excellent when roasted or baked, although they may be eaten raw.

Habitat and Distribution: The plants are found on mountain slopes and valleys, from Montana to Washington, south to California, Nevada, Utah and Colorado.   Apparently they are not found in Arizona and New Mexico.

Description: These are dwarf, non-hairy, perennial plants with fleshy roots. Even the stem is largely underground and sheathed by large, thin, dry, membranaceous, non-green bracts. The leaves are narrowly divided. The white flowers are in compound umbels.

115. *Pastinaca sativa* (1) (Carrot Family)
Parsnip

Preparation and Uses: This is a garden escapee which may be prepared and eaten in the same way as cultivated parsnips.

One frequently hears that when parsnips escape from cultivation and run wild, they become poisonous. This is never the case. Such stories probably arose from people who had mistaken the deadly Water Hemlock (*Cicuta* species) for wild parsnips.

Habitat and Distribution: Parsnip is found in damp places throughout the West.

Description: *P. sativa* is a tall, branching, stout, non-hairy biennial with pinnately compound leaves. The yellow flowers are in large umbels. The single, long, tap root is thick and fleshy. Do not confuse this with Water Hemlock which has a bundle of fleshy roots.

116. *Lomatium* species (62) (Carrot Family)
Biscuitroot

Preparation and Uses: All of the many species have edible roots. The green stems may be eaten in the spring, but as summer progresses, they become tough and fibrous. Tea may be made from the leaves, stems and flowers. The roots can be eaten raw, the taste resembling that of celery, or they may be peeled and the inside dried, then ground into flour. The flour is then mixed with water and kneaded until it is about the consistency of pie crust dough, flattened into cakes, and dried in the sun or baked; the resultant cakes taste like stale biscuits. Indians and early settlers made cakes about 2 feet long by a foot wide and left a hole in the middle to secure to saddle or pack, or to hang from the rafters of the dwelling.

The tiny seeds, though laborious to collect, are nutritious raw or roasted and can be dried and ground into flour.

Habitat and Distribution: *Lomatium* species are found in dry ground throughout the more arid portions of the West.

Description: These plants are perennials with thick roots. The leaves are several times divided, mostly from the base. The stem bearing the flower is leafless and short. The umbels are compound, usually terminal, sometimes partly lateral; the flowers are yellow, white, pink, or purplish.

117

*Lomatium
macrocarpum*
Large-fruited Biscuitroot

116

117. *Heracleum lanatum* (1) (Carrot Family)
Cowparsnip, Cowcabbage

Preparation and Uses: The cooked root tastes very much like rutabaga and is said to be good for the digestion, relieving one of gas, cramps, etc. It is also said to be effective in the treatment of epilepsy.

The young stems can be peeled and eaten raw, but are best when cooked. The hollow basal portion of the plant may be cut into short lengths, dried, and used as a substitute for salt by eating or cooking a piece with other food. The leaves may be dried and burned, and the ashes used as a salt substitute.

This plant is a member of the Parsley family and care should be taken to identify it positively since such similar-appearing plants as Water Hemlock (*Cicuta* species, all of which are deadly poisonous) are poisonous.

Habitat and Distribution: Cowparsnip is found in moist, often partially shaded ground throughout Western mountain areas, but also along the coast.

Description: The plant is a stout, conspicuous, perennial herb growing from 3 - 10 feet tall. The very large compound leaves have 3 coarsely toothed, ovate leaflets. The numerous white flowers form compound umbels, with the marginal flowers much larger than those toward the interior.

118. *Cornus canadensis* (1) (Dogwood Family)
Bunchberry

Preparation and Uses: The fruits may be eaten raw or cooked, and are reported to be good in puddings. This and other species such as *C. nuttallii* (Western Flowering Dogwood) may be used in other

118

121
Symphoricarpus mollis
Creeping Snowberry

119

120

ways including: a good, mildly stimulative, cold and fever remedy can be made by boiling the dried root or bark, the root being more potent, and then drinking a cupful of the mixture. The feathered bark makes a good toothbrush, said by old-timers to greatly brighten the teeth. The fresh bark is cathartic.

Habitat and Distribution: The various species are found in moist woods throughout the West, although *C. canadensis* is not found in Arizona.

Description: A typical dogwood, Bunchberry flowers appear to be solitary at the ends of their stems. Actually, the 4 large, white "petals" are really bracts surrounding a cluster of small, yellowish to purplish flowers. The flowering stems grow from 3 to 10 inches high or more, and bear oval, whorled leaves near the top, but beneath the flowers.

119. *Galium aparine* (1) (Madder Family)
Cleavers, Goosegrass Bedstraw

Preparation and Uses: The seeds may be roasted, ground, and used as a substitute for coffee, which they distinctly resemble in flavor. This is perhaps not surprising since this genus belongs in the same plant family as true coffee. It is probable that the seeds of other species in the genus have a coffee flavor. Since none of the species are listed as toxic it would probably be safe to experiment with them. The plants have a pleasant aroma when dried and were once used extensively for mattress-stuffing; hence the name of bedstraw. One species, *G. verum,* has the distinction of supposedly being the plant which filled the manger of the new-born Christ at Bethlehem. A purple dye may be obtained from the roots of many of the species.

Habitat and Distribution: Cleavers is found in many habitats. It is most common in moist areas, especially along streams, but is occasionally found in dry deserts. It may be found in wooded or open places up to elevations of 9500 feet in the Rockies; lower in the far West.

Description: The plant is a weak-stemmed, sprawling, spreading annual. The stems are sparsely branched and covered with backward curving, bristly hairs on the angles, and are hairy at the nodes. The thin, veiny, slender leaves occur in whorls of 6 - 8. The flowers are small, whitish, and are clustered 2 - 5 in the upper leaf axils. The fruits, containing the seeds, are covered with hooked bristles.

120. *Sambucus melanocarpa* and *caerulea*
(2) (Honeysuckle Family)
Elderberry, Black Elderberry,
Blackbead Elder

Preparation and Uses: The black or blue (depending on the species) fruit matures in late summer and is sweet and juicy, and makes excellent pies, jellies and wine. Some people experience nausea when eating the fruit raw, but cooking renders it safe to all.

The red fruited elderberries are reported poisonous from some localities, and edible from others. The author knows of one definite case of poisoning due to a red fruited variety.

Jelly is frequently made commercially from the black or blue fruited elderberries. The bark of these plants has been used in medicine as a diruetic and purgative.

Habitat and Distribution: Elderberries are found along streams and on mountain slopes throughout the West where there is adequate moisture.

Description: These plants are shrubs to small trees with pinnately compound, opposite leaves. The small white flowers are in compound cymes. The edible fruits are black or blue, the poisonous one bright red.

121. *Symphoricarpos* species (10) (Honeysuckle Family) Snowberry, Wolfberry

Preparation and Uses: The white, insipid berries are edible raw or cooked, although *S. racemosa* has been occasionally reported as mildly poisonous due to the quantity of saponin found in the berries.

Habitat and Distribution: Snowberries are found in woods and thickets, occasionally forming thickets themselves, throughout the West.

Description: The Snowberries are nearly prostrate to erect shrubs with simple, entire to toothed or lobed, opposite, deciduous leaves. The small, rose, white, pink, or purplish flowers are borne in few-flowered, terminal, or axillary racemes. The white berries are fleshy and have 2 nutlets within.

122. *Lonicera involucrata, ciliosa,* and *utahensis* (3) (Honeysuckle Family) Bearberry Honeysuckle, Honeysuckle, Twinberry

Preparation and Uses: The berries are pleasant tasting when eaten raw, and may be dried for future use.

Habitat and Distribution: These shrubs occur throughout the West in moist thickets, often along streams in open coniferous forest.

Description: The plants are upright shrubs, or vines with opposite entire leaves and paired yellow flowers. *L. involucrata* is shrubby and has dark

purple or black fruit. *L. ciliosa* is a trailing or woody vine with bright red berries. *L. utahensis* is a shrub with red fruit.

123. *Valeriana edulis* (1) (Valerian Family)
Valerian, Tobacco Root

Preparation and Uses: The roots of this and a few other species are ill smelling and ill tasting, but may be rendered quite palatable by long (24 hours) steaming in a stone-lined fire pit, or steamed by more modern methods. They may then be eaten as is, made into soup, or dried and ground into flour and made into bread. The seeds may be eaten raw but are best when parched.

These plants were an important food source to a number of western Indian groups. *V. officinalis* (Garden Heliotrope) is cultivated as a drug plant. Drugs obtained from it are used for treatment of nervous disorders and as mild stimulants.

Habitat and Distribution: Valerians are found in rich, moist soil in mountains throughout the West. *V. edulis* is not found in California.

Description: *V. edulis* is a perennial herb rising 1 to 2 feet high from a large, fleshy taproot. The leaves and stems are very smooth and entirely without hairs. The thick, textured leaves are erect, rather long and narrow, and number few to many at the base. The pinkish to white flowers are borne in long, narrow, panicles.

124. *Valerianella olitoria* and *carinata*
(2) (Valerian Family)
Corn Salad, Lamb's Lettuce

Preparation and Uses: The entire plant above ground may be eaten raw in salad.

Habitat and Distribution: Corn Salad is found in shady, often moist places in Washington, Oregon, California, Idaho, Montana, and Utah. Since it is an introduced plant (from Europe) it should be looked for in the remaining western states.

Description: The two plants listed above are quite similar, having branched stems and entire to partly lobed, more or less fleshy, opposite leaves. The small flowers are white to pale blue and are arranged in rather flattopped, bracted clusters. The flower is funnel-shaped.

125. *Balsamorhiza* species (9) (Sunflower Family) Balsamroot

Preparation and Uses: Although all the species are edible, the ones with the larger roots are to be preferred simply because of their size. These plants are particularly useful in that all of the plant may be used. The large root can be collected throughout the year, and eaten raw or, better, cooked in as many ways as the imagination can conceive. In spring the young stems and leaves may be eaten raw, in salads, or boiled as greens. As the stems and leaves grow older they remain edible but become tough and fibrous. The seeds are excellent when roasted and may be ground into a nutritious flour. When a cup of the flour is added to the recipe for a loaf of white bread, the result is delicious.

Habitat and Distribution: These plants are found in dry, often stony ground nearly throughout the West.

Description: They are perennial plants with large roots, the leaves being almost all basal with a few much smaller leaves on the upright stems. The large solitary heads are of sunflower-like yellow flowers.

126. *Helianthus annuus* and related species
(11) (Sunflower Family)
Sunflower

Preparation and Uses: These native plants provide dark gray seeds that are excellent when eaten raw or roasted. Various Indian tribes parched the seeds, ground them into meal and made nutritious bread and cakes. Some Indian groups actually cultivated the plant, and extracted oil from the seeds. Purple and black dyes were made from the seeds, and a yellow dye was boiled from the flowers. Sunflowers are cultivated the world over today, some varieties attaining heights of 20 feet, with flower heads of 1 foot or more across. The seeds are now used for human food, poultry feed, and pet food. Oil is extracted for use in cooking, in margarine, and in paints. The oil may be extracted by boiling the crushed seeds and then skimming the oil from the surface of the water. The roasted shells were once used as a coffee substitute. Seeds that have been heavily browned by roasting may also be used as a coffee substitute.

The Jerusalem Artichoke, *H. tuberosus,* is a sunflower with especially large, edible tubers. It was cultivated by some American Indian groups and was introduced into Europe where it has become extensively cultivated. The flesh is watery and sweet with a quite agreeable taste. The name "Jerusalem" is very misleading, and has nothing to do with that part of the world. The plant was early introduced to the Mediterranian area where the Italians called it girasole, and the Spanish, girasol. The English version of this was "Jerusalem."

The tubers of *H. maximilianii* may be eaten raw, roasted, or boiled, and the roots of others, such as *H. nuttallii* are nutritious, although somewhat fibrous.

*Balsamorhiza
sagittata*
Balsamroot

125

*Thelesperma
megapotamicum*
Greenthread

127

128

126a

Habitat and Distribution: Sunflowers are widely distributed in dry open ground throughout the West.

Description: The sunflowers are coarse, perennial or annual herbs with simple leaves that may be alternate or opposite. The flower heads are rather large, showy, and solitary, or a few in a bunch. The ray flowers are yellow and the disk flowers are yellow, purple, or brown. The disk flowers are complete with stamens and pistil, but the ray flowers have neither. The seeds are flattened and sometimes 4-angled.

127. *Thelesperma* species (3) (Sunflower Family)
Navajo Tea, Cota, Greenthread

Preparation and Uses: An excellent tea may be made by boiling the dried flowers and young leaves for several minutes.

Habitat and Distribution: The various species are found on dry hills, stream banks, grassy plains and mesas, open woodlands, slopes, and canyons of Wyoming, Colorado, Utah, New Mexico, Arizona, and Mexico.

Description: These plants are annual, biennial, or perennial herbs with opposite leaves that are linearally finely divided and rarely entire. The yellow flower heads are borne on long stalks.

128. *Madia glomerata* and *sativa*
(2) (Sunflower Family)
Cluster Tarweed, Tarweed

Preparation and Uses: The seeds may be eaten raw, roasted, dried, or ground into meal. When scalded the seeds yield a good, nutritious oil.

Habitat and Distribution: The Tarweeds are found in dry, open ground from Saskatchewan to British Columbia, south to California, northern Arizona and northern New Mexico.

Description: *M. glomerata* has a very rigid, very leafy, rather glandular stem. The leaves are narrowly linear. The greenish-yellow to purplish flowers are in dense heads. The seeds are compressed.

M. sativa has stout stems, often rigidly branched above, that are glandular well down toward the base. The flowers are pale yellow. The seeds are compressed.

129. *Grindelia* species (5) (Sunflower Family)
     Gum Plant, Gumweed, Rasinweed

Preparation and Uses: The dried or green leaves make a pleasing tea. The green leaves may be chewed. A broth of the leaves is said to relieve indigestion, and throat and lung troubles. If administered externally the broth will relieve itching and other skin irritations. Both Indians and pioneers used the plant in these ways. Today the dried flower heads and leaves of *G. squarrosa* provide an extract used in various medicines. All of the species are selenium absorbers.

Habitat and Distribution: *Grindelia* is one of the first plants to invade disturbed areas, such as roadsides. It is common in dry, open places throughout the West.

Description: The plants are mostly coarse, usually resinous, perennial herbs, although some are annual or biennial. The leaves are alternate and rather stiff. Most of the species have a taproot. The yellow flower heads are medium to large in size, and are not numerous.

132

130

131
Galinsoga parviflora
Quickweed

129
Grindelia squarrosa
Rasinweed

130. *Solidago missouriensis*
     (1) (Sunflower Family)
     Goldenrod

    Preparation and Uses: The young leaves are good as a potherb. The dried leaves and the dried, fully expanded flowers make good tea. An antiseptic lotion may be made from any of the species by boiling the stems and leaves. An antiseptic powder may be made by powdering dry, mature leaves.

    Goldenrod has a sap high in rubber content. Efforts have been made in the past to breed and cultivate this plant so as to have a domestic supply of natural rubber.

    Habitat and Distribution: Goldenrod is found in open pine forests and along streams throughout the West.

    Description: Goldenrod is a perennial herb with leafy stems rising from creeping rhizomes. The plant may be thickened and woody at the base. The alternate leaves are entire or toothed; both leaf types may be on the same plant. The yellow, radiate, flower heads are small and numerous.

131. *Galinsoga* species (3) (Sunflower Family)
     Quickweed

    Preparation and Uses: The entire young plant above ground may be used as a potherb.

    Habitat and Distribution: These natives of Mexico to South America have spread world-wide. They may be found growing in moist, open ground throughout the West, except, apparently, for Washington and Oregon.

    Description: The Quickweeds are annual herbs with leafy, branching, stems. The flowers occur in flattopped clusters. The ray flowers are white; the disk flowers are yellow. The oval, toothed, leaves are borne oppositely.

132. *Aster ledophyllus (Engelmannii)*
     (1) (Sunflower Family)
     White Aster, Aster

Preparation and Uses: The leaves may be boiled as greens. It is probable, but not known for sure, that other species are also edible.

Habitat and Distribution: The White Aster is found in moist to wet soil in open woods and grassy areas throughout the West.

Description: The plant is a several stemmed, perennial rising from 1 to 3 or 4 feet from a stout, woody base. The white to lavender-purple flowers are borne in a flattopped cluster. The 2 to 4 inch long leaves are oval to oblong, entire to toothed, a lighter green underneath than above, and rather thin, showing the veins in a network.

133. *Achillea lanulosa* (1) (Sunflower Family)
     Yarrow

Preparation and Uses: The entire plant above ground may be dried, boiled in water, strained and then administered to remedy a run-down condition or a disordered digestion. This brew also makes a rather nourishing broth.

A. millefolium is thought to contain some alkaloidal poison, so care should be exercised in the use of *A. lanulosa*. *A. millefolium* is a European species which has been introduced to the United States. It contains the drug *achilleine* which is sometimes used in acute suppression of the menses. It was once used as a tonic to treat urinary disorders. The Indians used our native Yarrow for various disorders. The plant imparts an unpleasant flavor to the milk of cattle that have eaten it. That famous Greek, Achilles, used a plant named

135

134

133

Achillea, which may have been a species of this genus, to treat the wounds of his warriors.

Habitat and Distribution: Yarrow is very common in dry pine forest and in sage along the edges of forests throughout the West. It is found as low as 2500 feet in California and as high as 11,000 feet in Colorado.

Description: The plant is a strongly scented perennial usually less than 2 feet high, entirely covered with dense, soft, more or less spreading hairs. The linear leaves are finely divided into numerous narrow divisions. The white flowers are in small numerous heads which in turn are in a dense, terminal, rather flattopped arrangement.

134. *Artemisia tridentata*
(27) (Sunflower Family)
Big Sagebrush

Preparation and Uses: Any of the 27 or so species may be used, but *A. tridentata* is the best. The seeds or fruits may be dried, pounded into meal to make pinole, or eaten raw.

Several species were used medicinally by western Indians and early white settlers. *A. mexicana* produces the drug *santonin,* used in treatment of roundworm infections. The Hopi Indians formerly roasted the leaves of *A. frigida* with corn to flavor it. The oil in the foliage of a number of the sages is used in the manufacture of absinthe. Tea made from the leaves was once used in the treatment of colds, sore eyes, and as a hair tonic. The author knows one old-timer in Wyoming who still makes hair tonic from it.

Habitat and Distribution: This plant is characteristic of the Great Basin Desert and is found in arid habitats throughout the West.

Description: Sage is easily recognized by the silvery-gray color of the leaves and their familiar aromatic sage odor. They range from herbaceous plants to large woody shrubs. The leaves are alternate and may have from none to 3 clefts. The flowers are in heads, are small, and are yellow or yellowish-white.

135. *Petasites speciosa* and related species
(4) (Sunflower Family)
Sweet Coltsfoot, Western Coltsfoot,
Butter Bur

Preparation and Uses: The young foliage and flowers make a good potherb. A good salt substitute may be made by rolling the green leaves and stems into balls, drying them, burning them, and using the ashes as salt.

Habitat and Distribution: The Coltsfoot is found in damp, shaded ground throughout the West, except, apparently, for Arizona and New Mexico.

Description: The plants are herbaceous perennials with a thick, creeping rootstock, from which rises a leafless stem. The large, long-petioled leaves are basal and covered underneath with short, densely matted, soft, white, woolly hairs.

136. *Antennaria* species
(28) (Sunflower Family)
Pussytoes

Preparation and Uses: The gum of the stalks can be chewed to make a pleasing gum claimed to be somewhat nourishing.

Habitat and Distribution: Pussytoes are found mainly in arid, mountainous country throughout the West. However, the habitats vary widely as one

*Antennaria
rosea*
Pussytoes
136

species is found along streams.

Description: The plants are woolly, primarily small or moderate sized, mostly herbaceous, perennial, and with pistillate and staminate flowers on separate plants.   The leaves are alternate and entire.   The heads are solitary or in clusters; the flowers are whitish.   Staminate plants in many of the species are rare or unknown; the pistillate plants mature their seeds without fertilization.

137.   *Arctium minus* and *lappa*
       (2) (Sunflower Family)
       Burdock

Preparation and Uses: Both of these plants were introduced from Europe.   Various species of this group grow wild, and are cultivated widely over the world, especially in the Orient.   In the West, *A. minus* is by far the more common of the species.

The root is quite pithy and has a tough rind that must be peeled away.   After peeling, the root should be boiled in 2 waters - the first with soda to soften it, and the second with salt and other seasonings for flavor.

The young leaves may be boiled and eaten.   The young stems and flower stalk may be peeled down to the pith and can then be included with the leaves. Here again, to remove strong taste, cooking in two waters is often advisable.   The pith of young stems may be eaten raw in salads, or it may be pickled or candied.

Habitat and Distribution: These plants are found in moist soil in many areas of the West.

Description: The Burdocks are coarse biennials with large, petioled leaves and thick stems.   The flower heads number from several to many, and are pink to purple in color. The fruit develops into a tenacious bur, hence the common name of Burdock.

138. *Cirsium* species (31) (Sunflower Family)
Thistle, Canadian Thistle, Elk Thistle

Preparation and Uses: The many species all have roots that may be eaten raw, boiled or roasted. They are nutritious, although somewhat flat in taste. The peeled stems may be cooked as greens.

Habitat and Distribution: Thistles are found in many habitats; grassy meadows, the openings in coniferous woods, or dry waste places throughout the West.

Description: The plants are biennial or perennial herbs. They are often woolly with spiny bracts surrounding the flowers and spiny leaves. The leaves are alternate and toothed or lobed. The flowerheads are rather large, purple, pink, red, or sometimes yellowish or white.

139. *Carduus* species (4) (Sunflower Family)
Plumeless Thistle, Italian Thistle,
Bristle Thistle

Preparation and Uses: The pith, without the easily removable rind, may be boiled in salted water and seasoned in various ways, after which it is quite flavorful. The dried flowers may be used as a rennet to curdle milk.

Habitat and Distribution: These thistles are weedy plants found along roadsides and in other open ground throughout the West.

Description: Refer to the description for *Cirsium*, since these thistles are extremely similar. The main difference is that the "thistle-down" (pappus bristles) is simple and smoothish in *Carduus*, instead of plumed, as in *Cirsium*.

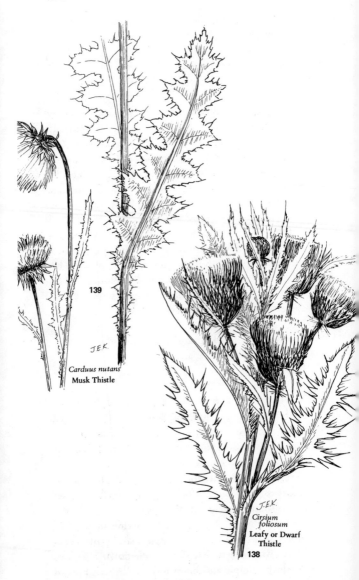

J.E.K.

Carduus nutans
Musk Thistle

139

J.E.K.
*Cirsium
foliosum*
**Leafy or Dwarf
Thistle**
138

140. *Cichorium intybus* (1) (Sunflower Family)
Chicory, Chicory Lettuce

Preparation and Uses: The leaves may be eaten raw or cooked like spinach. The root may also be eaten raw, but is best when boiled or roasted. The root may be dried and ground and used as a good substitute for coffee.

Habitat and Distribution: Chicory is a European introduction widely found throughout the West in roadsides, fields and waste places.

Description: The plant is a perennial with stiff, rather rigid, short-branched stems rising from 1-4 feet above a large taproot. The stems are covered with minute stiff hairs. The basal leaves are 3-6 inches or more long and in a spreading basal rosette. They are pinnately lobed to entire, oblanceolate, often with reddish petioles and midveins. The upper leaves are much smaller, with basal lobes and entire margins. The flower heads are deep blue, numerous, showy, 1 inch or more across, and usually sessile.

141. *Microseris nutans* (1) (Sunflower Family)
Nodding Microseris

Preparation and Uses: The small roots are best when eaten raw.

Habitat and Distribution: The plant is found on plains and in dry open woods from British Columbia, south into California, and east to the Rockies.

Description: Nodding Microseris is a slender, perennial herb, 4 to 12 inches high, with from one to several stems rising from thickened roots. The entire, toothed or pinnately lobed leaves are on the lower part of the stem. The solitary heads are composed of yellow flowers that have strap-shaped corollas.

142. *Lygodesmia juncea* (1) (Sunflower Family)
      Skeleton Weed

   Preparation and Uses: Indians prepared a satisfy-
ing chewing gum from this plant by cutting the
stems into pieces so that the sap would escape;
when this coagulated, it was collected and chewed.

   Habitat and Distribution: Skeleton Weed is
found in dry ground on plains, hills, and valleys in
eastern Washington, Idaho, Montana, Colorado,
Utah, eastern Nevada, Wyoming, and New Mexico.
It is apparently not found at all in Oregon, California, and Arizona.

   Description: This is a perennial plant with deeply buried rootstocks. The lower leaves are linear,
ascending, firm to the touch, and entire. The upper leaves are scale-like. The stems are stiff, highly
branched, and are often swollen by gummy, globe-
shaped galls. The flowers are rose to pink in color.

143. *Lygodesmia grandiflora* (1) (Sunflower Family)
      Rush-Pink

   Preparation and Uses: The Hopi Indians of
Arizona boiled the leaves of this plant with meat or
mush. They believe that it can stimulate milk flow
in women.

   Habitat and Distribution: Rush-Pink is found in
dry, sandy or gravelly soil, often among grasses
throughout the West except for Washington, Oregon, California, and western Nevada.

   Description: This is a perennial plant with deep-
seated rootstocks, and tall, usually leafy stems
with conspicuous, linear, entire, grasslike leaves.
The large, showy, rose or pink flowers occur at the
ends of the stems.

144. *Tragopogon* species (4) (Sunflower Family)
Goatsbeard, Salsify, Oyster Plant

Preparation and Uses: The fleshy roots may be eaten raw or cooked, tasting like oysters or parsnips, according to whom you are speaking. When only a few inches high the young stems, along with the bases of the lower leaves may be used as potherbs.

The coagulated milky juice of these introduced plants was used for chewing by various Indian groups. The juice was considered a remedy for indigestion. In olden times in Greece, Italy, and other Old World areas linen pads were soaked in the distilled juice and applied to bleeding sores and wounds. Pliny records that the juice, when mixed with woman's milk, is a cure-all for disorders of the eyes. *T. porrifolius* is the cultivated Salsify or Oyster Plant.

Habitat and Distribution: The Goatsbeards are found in open ground throughout the West.

Description: These plants are tall, stout, biennial or perennial herbs with fleshy tap-roots, and entire, grasslike, clasping leaves. The yellow or purple flower heads are borne on tall, leafy stems: the matured head resembling a fluffy, giant, dandelion head.

145. *Lactuca tatarica* and related species
(9) (Sunflower Family)
Chicory Lettuce, Wild Lettuce

Preparation and Uses: The gum of the roots may be used for chewing. The entire young plant above ground, and the leaves of older plants, may be eaten raw in salads or cooked as greens. After flowering they become rather tough. *L. sativa* is common garden lettuce.

145

146

144

Tragopogon dubius
Yellow Salsify

Habitat and Distribution: The plants are found in moist ground widely distributed through the West.

Description: The various species are annual or perennial, leafy-stemmed, herbs bearing mostly panicled heads. The flowers number few to many. The plants have the typical milky sap expected in lettuce.

146. *Sonchus asper* (1) (Sunflower Family)
Prickly Sow-Thistle

Preparation and Uses: The stems and leaves, especially the young ones, may be used as greens. A gum obtained from a related species *(S. oleraceus)* has been used as a "cure" for opium addiction.

Habitat and Distribution: Sow Thistle is an abundant weed in open ground throughout the West.

Description: Sow Thistle is leafy-stemmed with a milky juice. The stems are smooth and covered with a waxy powdery substance, and are 1 to 5 feet high with prickly toothed leaves. The yellow flowers occur in heads and all are strap-shaped. The leaves are generally not lobed, but the margins support sharp, needle-like teeth.

147. *Hieracium* species (21) (Sunflower Family)
Hawkweed

Preparation and Uses: The green plants and their coagulated juice make a satisfactory substitute for chewing gum, and were so used by Western Indians, especially those of the Northwest.

The genus is world-wide, comprising perhaps as many as 300 species. The ancients in the Old World believed that hawks ate the sap to sharpen their eyesight.

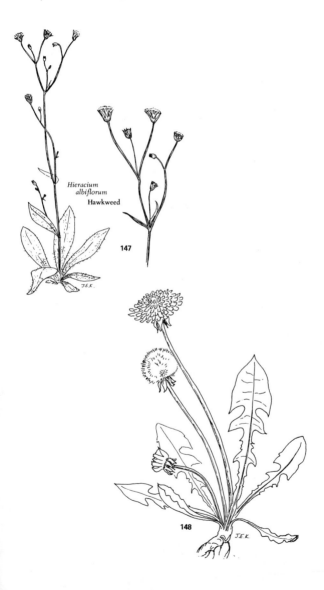

*Hieracium
albiflorum*
Hawkweed

147

148

150

149

Habitat and Distribution: Hawkweed is found on hills and mountains, often in woods, throughout the West.

Description: The Hawkweeds are perennial herbs, often hairy, sometimes glandular, with alternate or all basal leaves. The flower heads are usually several in number, rarely solitary, and are yellow or white. All the flowers have strap-shaped corollas.

148. *Taraxacum officinale* and related species
(5) (Sunflower Family)
Dandelion

Preparation and Uses: The leaves may be eaten raw or cooked. Often they are bitter and need to be boiled in two or more waters to remove the bitter taste. The roots may be eaten raw in salads or cooked in stew. The roots also have a medicinal effect and have been used for centuries throughout the world as a tonic, mild laxative, and diuretic. The roasted root has been used as a substitute for coffee. A good wine may be made from the flower heads.

Although the species listed above is a native of the Old World it has become widely established in the United States. We also have several native species with similar qualities.

Habitat and Distribution: Dandelion is found throughout the West wherever there is sufficient moisture.

Description: These common and well-known plants are biennial or perennial herbs, with leaves appearing as a basal rosette or tuft from the center of which rises a showy, yellow, flower head.

149. *Lapsana communis* (1) (Sunflower Family)
Nipplewort

152

Alisma triviale
Water Plantain
151

Preparation and Uses: The young plants that have not yet flowered may be eaten raw in salad. Nipplewort is best cooked, however.

Habitat and Distribution: This weed is a native of Europe and is widely scattered over the West in waste places and along roadsides; it is apparently not found in Arizona.

Description: Nipplewort is a slender, branching, erect annual bearing alternate, oval, toothed leaves. The yellow flower heads are arranged in panicles.

150.   *Sagittaria latifolia* and related species
       (5) (Water Plantain Family)
       Arrowhead, Duckpotato, Tulepotato,
       Wappato

Preparation and Uses: All of the species produce starchy, white tubers at the end of the rootstocks, which may place them several feet away from the parent plant. The entire root is edible but usually only the tubers are worth collecting. Roasted or boiled, they are superior to potatoes.

The genus is found world-wide and in Asia the various available species are an important food source, often being cultivated at the edges of rice paddies. Occasionally the tubers are seen on sale in Chinese sections of our larger cities here in the United States.

In the Pacific Northwest the Indian method of collection (performed by the women) was to wade into a pond where the plants were growing and feel for the tubers in the mud with their toes. After being dislodged in this way the tubers would float to the surface where they were easily collected. Since the tubers are best developed in late summer or autumn this often necessitated wading neck-deep in icy water. If the Indian woman was lucky she might come upon a muskrat's collected store of the tubers and obtain a bushel or more at one time.

Habitat and Distribution: Arrowhead is found in ponds or very wet ground throughout the West.

Description: These plants are mostly aquatic or marsh perennial herbs, bearing tubers on the roots, and containing a milky sap throughout. The leaf blades are lanceolate or arrowhead-shaped, hence the common name. The leaves may be floating on the water surface or held erect above it. The white flowers are in whorls of 3.

151. *Alisma* species (2) (Water Plantain Family)
Water Plantain, Mud Plantain

Preparation and Uses: The starchy, bulbous bases of the plant are edible. They have a very strong taste when fresh and should be allowed to dry thoroughly, after which they may be used as a starchy vegetable.

Habitat and Distribution: The taxonomy of this genus appears somewhat confused, at least here in the West. It is probable that there are only 2 species, *A. triviale* and *A. geyeri,* and they both are found throughout the West in habitats varying from aquatic to moist, boggy meadows.

Description: These plants are perennial herbs with basal, several-ribbed, erect or floating leaves. The numerous, small, white to pinkish flowers are in panicles of whorled branches. The stamens are 6 in number.

152. *Potamogeton natans* and related species
(10) (Pondweed Family)
Pondweed

Preparation and Uses: Although there are many

more than 10 species, there are only 10 or so that have rootstocks large enough to be worth bothering with, if any are, since one must get wet to gather the edible rootstocks. However, when the weather is warm collecting them can be fun. The younger branches of the roots are more starchy than the older and can be boiled with meat, steamed, etc.

Habitat and Distribution: These plants are found in ponds and quiet streams throughout the West.

Description: The pondweeds are immersed aquatic herbs with leafy stems. The leaves are alternate; sometimes the upper ones being opposite. The floating leaves are usually much broader than the submerged ones, which are often quiet slender, and with stipules.   The flowers are axillary.

153. *Triglochin maritima* (1) (Arrow-weed Family)
Arrow Grass, Sourgrass, Goosegrass

Preparation and Uses: The seeds were parched and ground into flour by several western Indian groups. When roasted, the seeds were used by early western pioneers as a substitute for coffee.

The plants, especially in times of drought, often contain toxic quantities of hydrocyanic acid and have caused much death in livestock. The seeds are rendered safe by parching or roasting since the poison is quite volatile.

Habitat and Distribution: Arrow Grass is abundant in salt marshes along the coast and elsewhere, and in alkaline meadows throughout the West.

Description: Arrow Grass is a slender, unbranched, densely tufted plant, rising from 1 to 3 feet high from short, thick rootstocks. The grasslike, fleshy leaves are all basal, and are round on one side and flat on the other. The small flowers are in terminal racemes which, when mature, bear rather flat, strongly ridged seeds.

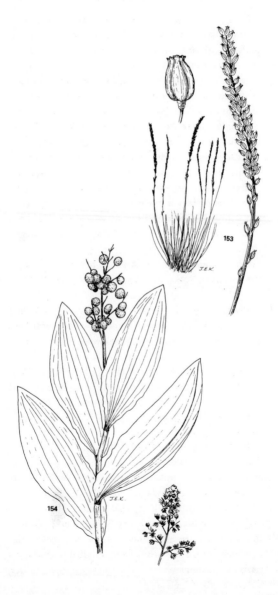

154. *Smilacina racemosa* and related species
(5) (Lily Family)
False Solomon Seal

Preparation and Uses: *S. racemosa* has starchy, aromatic rootstocks that may be eaten. They should first be soaked overnight in lye to remove the bitterness, then parboiled to remove the lye. The rootstocks also make a good pickle. The young shoots can be eaten as a potherb.

The berries of all species are edible but purgative if eaten in too great a quantity. Anyone with loose bowels should not eat the berries. Cooking the bitter-sweet berries removes much of the purgative element, and renders them much more palatable.

Habitat and Distribution: These plants are found in rich, moist, soil in coniferous forests throughout the West.

Description: A leafy, unbranched stem rises from strong rootstocks and ends in a dense raceme of whitish to greenish flowers. The large, ovate leaves have heavy, prominent veins. The berry is usually red or greenish-red with small purple spots.

155. *Streptopus amplexifolius* (1) (Lily Family)
Twistedstalk, Liverberry

Preparation and Uses: The red, juicy berries may be eaten raw or cooked in soups and stews. *S. curvipes* is probably edible too, but there is no definite record of its edible qualities, and the author has not tried it.

In some localities Twistedstalk is reported to be somewhat cathartic, but not so in other areas. If one has loose bowels it is probably wise to partake lightly of this berry.

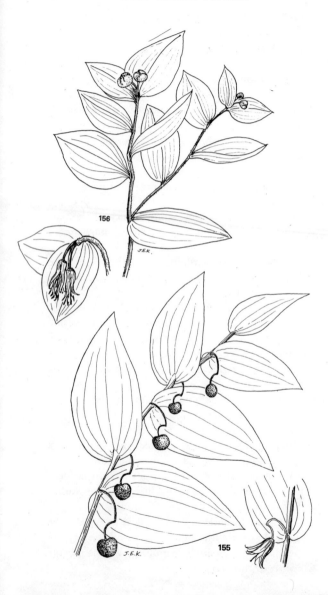

Habitat and Distribution: Twistedstalk is found in moist woods throughout the West.

Description: This plant is a perennial herb rising from horizontal rootstocks. The small, greenish or yellowish flowers are borne in the leaf axils and have a distinct twist or kink near the middle of their stalk. The oval-lanceolate leaves have no petioles and appear to almost wrap around the stem at the leaf base. The leaves are strongly veined.

156. *Disporum trachycarpum* (1) (Lily Family)
Fairybells, Disporum

Preparation and Uses: The sweet tasting yellow or orange berries were eaten raw by the Blackfoot Indians. Avoid picking the flowers, as they are beautiful additions to our woods.

Habitat and Distribution: Fairybells are found in rich damp soil of woods and brush throughout the West.

Description: A low, somewhat hairy, branched herb with sessile, ovate to oblong leaves 1 - 3 inches long. The yellowish-white flowers are solitary or 2 to 3 in drooping clusters at the ends of the branches. The stems reach 1 - 2 feet in height. The fruit is orange or yellow-orange, globose, velvet-skinned, and lobed.

157. *Asparagus officinalis* (1) (Lily Family)
Asparagus, Garden Asparagus

Preparation and Uses: This is ordinary Asparagus which often escapes cultivation. Use the young shoots.

Habitat and Distribution: The plant is widely established in moist ground throughout the farming areas of the West.

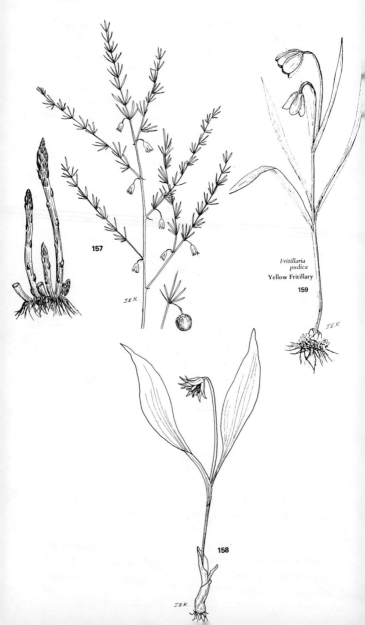

Fritillaria pudica
Yellow Fritillary
159

157

158

Description: The young shoots rise from the ground as simple stems, but later become tall and highly branched. The minute leaves are scalelike. The small, nodding flowers are greenish white and develop into a bright red berry. When mature, Asparagus is often used as a table decoration.

158. *Erythronium grandiflorum* (1) (Lily Family)
Yellow Fawn Lily

Preparation and Uses: The bulbs may be boiled and eaten or dried and stored. The leaves and fresh green seed pods may be used as greens. It is reported that the bulb of another member of this genus in Asia and Europe was boiled by the Tartars in broth or milk.

Habitat and Distribution: The plant is found in shaded woods, rich soil, moist streambanks and mountain meadows throughout the West.

Description: A single naked stem and 2 leaves rise from a deep set bulb. The leaves sheathe the base of the stem which rises from 4 - 10 inches high and bears one or more bright yellow, nodding flowers.

159. *Fritillaria* species (19) (Lily Family)
Fritillary

Preparation and Uses: Several members of this genus are cultivated as ornamentals, one of the most popular being called "Missionbells." The bulbs of all the species may be eaten raw or boiled and are good when dried. However, *F. meleagris,* a European introduction occasionally found in rock gardens, is said to have caused poisoning in Europe. It is thought to contain a heart-depressant alkaloid. Our native species of *F. atropurpurea* (Leopard

Lily, Mission-Bell, Purple Fritillary) and *F. pudica* (Yellowbell, Yellow Fritillary) are well known to be edible. Probably with some of the lesser known species care should be taken as to their ingestion as the body may require some orientation before it can handle larger quantities. Since these are all very beautiful flowers, they should be used for food only in an emergency.

Habitat and Distribution: The various species are found mainly in dry, open woods, slopes, fields and meadows throughout the West.

Description: This member of the lily family has leafy, unbranched stems arising from a fleshy-scaled bulb. The leaves are whorled or alternate, or both. The flowers are usually large and showy, in racemes or solitary. The petals and sepals are both showy, in racemes or solitary. The petals and sepals are both flower-like and similar, each with a gland near the base. The stamens number 6.

160. *Lilium* species (16) (Lily Family)
Lily

Preparation and Uses: All of the true lilies have edible bulbs, but because of their relative rarity and beauty they should not be harvested except in great emergency. The bulbs may be eaten raw or cooked, and have an excellent flavor. Throughout Asia various lilies are cultivated for their edible bulbs.

Lilies have long held man's interest and wonder, and much superstition has evolved about them. The lily, as long ago as several thousand years or more B.C., was believed to encourage virtue and purity. There is a legend that relates how in ancient times a Korean hermit removed an arrow from a wounded tiger and the two became friends as a result of this kindness. The tiger asked that when he should die the hermit use his magic to maintain their friend-

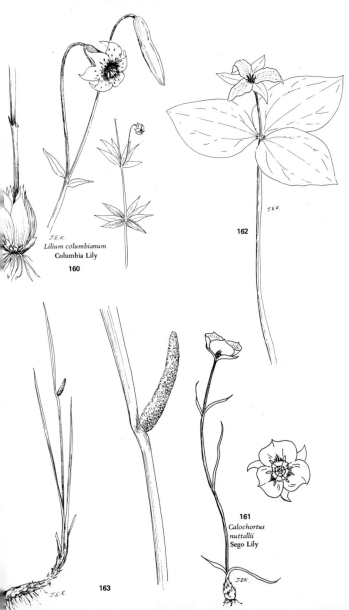

J.E.K.
Lilium columbianum
Columbia Lily
160

162

161
Calochortus nuttallii
Sego Lily

163

ship. The hermit agreed and when the tiger died his body became the Tiger Lily. Eventually the hermit was drowned and his body washed away. The Tiger Lily spread throughout the land looking for his friend.

Another legend tells how the originally yellow Madonna Lily became white when the Virgin Mary picked it, and has remained so ever since as evidence of that occurrence. Our own folklore contains stories, no doubt imported from Europe, of how close sniffing of lilies will cause freckles to appear.

Habitat and Distribution: The various species are found in dry to moist, open to shady, ground throughout the West.

Description: Lilies are perennial herbs with scaly bulbs or rootstocks. The simple stems are tall and leafy. The narrow, sessile leaves are alternate or in whorls. The flowers are large and showy, and vary from solitary to many on a terminal raceme. The flowers vary from funnel-shaped to bell-shaped. The stamens number 6.

161.   *Calochortus* species (40) (Lily Family)
Sego Lily, Mariposa Lily, Cat's Ear

Preparation and Uses: The bulbs are excellent when eaten raw and the flavor is improved by slowly steaming masses of them in fire pits, or by roasting them over a smoky fire. They also may be dried and ground into flour. Because these flowers are very beautiful, they should not be picked unless really needed.

The most famous species of this genus is *C. nuttallii*, the Sego Lily, which is Utah's state flower. Mormon pioneers made much use of this plant as a source of food.

Habitat and Distribution: The Sego Lilies are

found in open woods, valleys, and elsewhere in dry to moist ground throughout the West.

Description: Flowering stems rise from coated bulbs. The stems are simple or sparingly branched. The leaves are few, alternate and narrow. The flowers are few in a terminal cluster, or else solitary and quite showy, ranging in color from pale yellow to nearly scarlet and from white to deep lavender. The outermost flower parts are green and sepal-like. The stamens number 6.

162. *Trillium ovatum* and related species
     (4) (Lily Family)
     Wake Robin, Trillium

Preparation and Uses: The plant may be boiled as greens but because of its beauty and scarcity the collector should refrain from using it except in emergency. The root is a powerful emetic and was used by some western Indian groups as a presumed aid to birth. There are scattered, but not authenticated, reports of the berries also being emetic.

Habitat and Distribution: Wake Robin is found in moist, wooded areas throughout the West.

Description: The plants are low, hairless, unbranched perennials rising with stout stems from short, fleshy rootstocks. The stem bears a whorl of 3 leaves at the top. The beautiful pink, purple or yellow, solitary flower springs from the center of the leaf whorl.

163. *Acorus calamus* (1) (Iris Family)
     Sweet Flag

Preparation and Uses: The tender, young, inner shoots that appear in spring make a good salad. The rootstock may be candied by cutting it into small pieces and boiling for 2 or 3 days with several

changes of water, after which it should be boiled
for about 15 minutes in heavy sugar syrup.

Habitat and Distribution: Sweet Flag is found in
shallow water to wet ground along edges of ponds,
lakes, and streams. It has been reported from northern Idaho, north-central Colorado, the Blue Lake
area in Humboldt County, California, and from
Montana.

Description: One must be careful not to confuse this plant with the poisonous iris, to which it
is similar in appearance. Sweet Flag is ordinarily a
much larger plant, with erect, linear, yellow-green
leaves reaching 6 feet in length and having a width
of ½ to ¾ inch. The bruised leaves are aromatic.
The stem leaves are 2-ranked. The plant develops a
spathe, which in this case appears as a leaf-like extension of the stem.

164. *Sparganium eurycarpum* and *angustifolium*
     (2) (Bur Reed Family)
     Bur Reed

Preparation and Uses: The bulbous base of the
stem, and the tubers of the rhizomes, are edible
when cooked.

Plants of this genus were used in the Old World.
Dioscorides, a Greek physician (40 - 70 A.D.),
claimed that the root and seed of Bur Reed drunk
in wine helped neutralize snake bite.

Habitat and Distribution: Bur Reed is widely
distributed in swamps throughout the West.

Description: These plants are perennial aquatic
herbs rising from creeping rhizomes with simple or
branched, leafy stems. The stems and their alternate, elongate leaves may be found floating on the
water surface or erect above it. The sexes are separate in the flowers, with densely crowded, globose,

male flower heads being located above similarly arranged female flower heads.

165. *Typha* species (4) (Cattail Family)
Cattail

Preparation and Uses: All species of this genus bear edible roots containing a core of almost pure starch, as much as corn, in fact, and with less fat. The roots may be boiled or roasted, or dried and then ground into meal or flour. Bread may be made from the pollen and the young shoots are good raw or cooked.

Pioneers once used the leaves for caulking barrels and making rush-bottomed furniture. Indians used cattail down in dressings for wounds, in padding cradleboards, and both Indians and Whites used it for stuffing pillows.

Habitat and Distribution: The cattail is a familiar plant found in swamps, ponds, edges of streams and other marshy habitats throughout the West.

Description: Cattails are tall marsh perennials with light green, soft, pithy leaves. The flowers are in a dense, cylindrical, brown spike on a very long, stout peduncle.

166. *Allium* species (64) (this includes the cultivated onion) (Amaryllis Family)
Wild Onion

Preparation and Uses: All of the *Allium* species are known to be edible; their bulbs vary in degree of onion odor and flavor. The bulbs may be eaten raw, boiled, steamed, creamed, in soup, and are especially good when used as seasoning. They last well when stored for winter use. It should be remembered that ingestion of huge amounts of

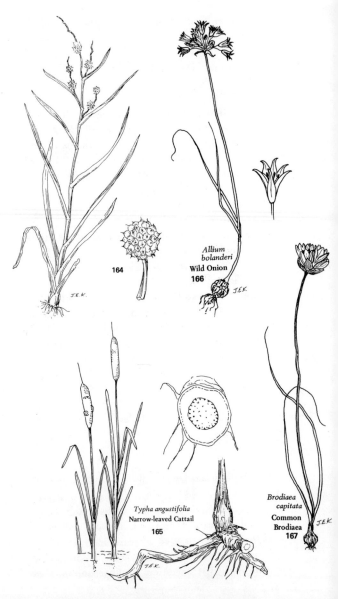

164

*Allium
bolanderi*
Wild Onion
166

Typha angustifolia
Narrow-leaved Cattail
165

*Brodiaea
capitata*
**Common
Brodiaea**
167

onions, including cultivated onions, can cause poisoning. It is thought that onions contain an alkaloid, but it is perfectly safe to eat normal amounts of wild onions in the same manner as cultivated onions.

Habitat and Distribution:　Wild onions are found distributed in moist ground throughout the West.

Description:　Wild onions are all herbaceous plants with basal leaves. A few basal leaves sheath the base of the flower stalk. The leaves are usually few in number and slender, but sometimes broad. The flowers are at the end of the stalk and are borne in a head below which are several tissue-like bracts. Together, the sepals and petals number six. The leaves and stalks have a characteristic onion flavor and odor.

167.　*Brodiaea* species (30) (Amaryllis Family)
　　　Brodiaea, Harvest Brodiaea, Wild Onion

Preparation and Uses:　The bulbs of the many species are edible raw, but are somewhat mucilaginous. Their flavor is improved if boiled slowly for a few minutes. They are at their best when roasted slowly in hot ashes for a half hour to an hour, during which time they become rather sweet. The young seed pods of *B. douglasii* may be used as greens.

Habitat and Distribution:　*Brodiaea* species are widely distributed through the West in dry open ground. Some species prefer moist soil.

Description:　The plants are perennial herbs with short, bulblike, underground stems. The leaves are all basal, mostly few and slender. The flowers are in an umbel-like cluster.

168.　*Habenaria dilatata* and related species
　　　(10) (Orchid Family)
　　　White Bog Orchid, Orchid, Rein Orchid

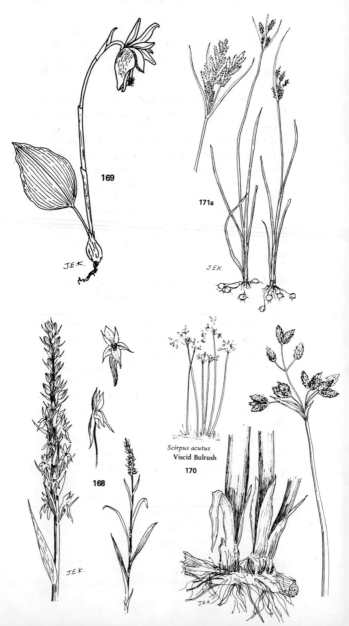

Scirpus acutus
Viscid Bulrush
170

Preparation and Uses: The tuberlike roots of these orchids may be eaten raw or cooked. However, since orchids are rare they should not be used unless one definitely has need for emergency food.

Habitat and Distribution: The majority of the species are found in moist to wet, boggy areas, but some do occur in dry ground. The genus is spread throughout the West.

Description: These orchids are perennial herbs with clustered, fleshy, tuberlike roots from which rise simple, leafy stems. Both basal and stem leaves sheathe the stem with their lower part; there is no petiole. The small, greenish to yellowish to waxy white flowers are borne in a terminal spike or raceme.

169. *Calypso bulbosa* (1) (Orchid Family)
Fairy Slipper, Lady Slipper, Venus Slipper

Preparation and Uses: This plant is rather rare and should not be harvested unless you have a desperate need for survival. The small bulb is quite tasty when eaten raw, roasted or boiled.

Habitat and Distribution: *Calypso bulbosa* is found in moist woods throughout the West.

Description: It is a low herbaceous plant with a single, broad leaf at the base of the stem. The stem is 2 to 7 inches high, the flower showy and slipper like. The 3 sepals and 2 upper petals are similar and colored rose to reddish purple. The lower petal forms a sac-like or slipper-like lip.

170. *Scirpus* species (22) (Sedge Family)
Bulrush, Tule

Preparation and Uses: Although the roots of all species are edible, some are better than others. The roots are quite starchy and may be eaten raw or baked, dried, or ground into a nutritious white flour.   Young roots, when crushed and boiled, yield a sweet syrup.

The pollen may be gathered, pressed into cakes, and baked. The seeds may be used whole, parched, ground, in mush, etc. The base of the stems and particularly the young autumn stemtips next to the ground may be eaten raw and are quite thirst-quenching. The long leaves were used by Indians in mat-weaving.

Habitat and Distribution: Bulrushes are found in wet ground, and on swamp, pond, and lake edges throughout the West.

Description: Bulrushes are mostly perennial, rarely annual, herbs. The hollow or pithy stems are erect and triangular to circular in cross-section, and bear leaves, or if not, the leaves are reduced to basal sheaths. The flowers are in heads, spikes, umbels, or sometimes in solitary spikelets.

171. *Cyperus esculentus* and *C. rotundus*
      (2) (Sedge Family)
      Yellow Nut Grass, Nut Grass

Preparation and Uses: The roots of these two species bear small, nutlike, underground tubers which have a pleasant nutty flavor when eaten raw.

C. esculentus is widely distributed throughout the world and is today cultivated in the South and in Europe for food. Both plants are troublesome weeds in irrigated land in Arizona.

Habitat and Distribution: Found in moist, but not swampy, ground throughout the West.

Description: *C. esculentus* is a perennial herb with the culms (stems) rising 1 to 2 feet tall from tuber-bearing roots. The grasslike leaves arise near the base, are light green, are about as long as the stem, and have a prominent midrib. Three to six smaller leaves form an involucre around the flower cluster, which has 5 to 8 rays. The spikelets are straw-colored, flat, spreading, many flowered, and numerous.

C. rotundus is very similar to *C. esculentus* but with shiny, reddish-brown scales.

172. *Glyceria* species (7) (Grass Family)
Manna Grass, Sugar Grass

Preparation and Uses: The seeds produce an excellent flour when parched and ground. They may also be boiled whole in the manner of rice, or added to soups or stews.

Habitat and Distribution: Manna Grasses are found throughout the West in aquatic or marshy habitats.

Description: The plants are mostly tall perennials with creeping underground stems. The leaves are very narrow, flat, and elongated, often floating on the water's surface. The silvery green, few to many flowered spikelets are in open or contracted panicles. The lemmas are broad, convex on the back, thin and dry at the tip and have 5 - 9 prominent veins.

173. *Phragmites communis* (1) (Grass Family)
Carrizo, Reed Grass, Reed

Preparation and Uses: The roots may be eaten raw, roasted, or boiled like potatoes. The young shoots and leaves may be boiled as a potherb. An excellent pickle may be made from the young shoot just above the root where it has not been exposed to the light. The seeds are quite nutritious and may be dried and ground into flour, or boiled whole, hull and all.

Various Indian groups, mostly Eastern, made a confection from the young, sugary stems of this plant. The shoots were gathered before blooming, dried, and then ground into flour and sifted for the

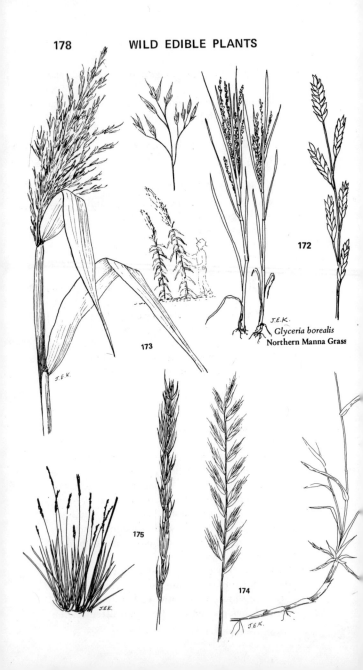

J.E.K.
Glyceria borealis
Northern Manna Grass

172

173

175

174

finer material which was mixed with water to make a thick, sweet, sticky dough. This was baked or roasted until slightly brown and then eaten.

Besides its uses as food, southwestern Indians used the reed for arrow shafts, prayer sticks, weaving-rods, mats, screens, pipestems, cordage, nets, thatching, and in some localities, fishing poles. String may be made by simply twisting together the fibers obtained from the reeds.

Habitat and Distribution: Reed Grass is found in swampy ground throughout the West.

Description: The plant is a perennial with jointed, stout, leafy, hollow or pithy stems 6 to 12 feet high when mature, with the flowers in large terminal panicles. The stems rise from long creeping rhizomes. The axes of the 3 to 7 flowered spikelets are covered with long silky hairs. The leaves are about 1 inch across.

174. *Agropyron repens* (1) (Grass Family)
     Quack Grass, Wheat Grass

Preparation and Uses: The rootstocks may be dried and ground, and the meal made into bread, or used in other ways.

Habitat and Distribution: This grass is a weed introduced from Europe, and is found in waste places throughout the West.

Description: Quack Grass grows to 3 feet high from rootstocks that are distinctively yellow-green in color. The flowering stems are either held erect or curve up from the base. The leaf blades are thin, flat, and linear, and bear short hairs on the upper surface.

175. *Elymus triticoides* and related species (12)
     (Grass Family)
     Wild Rye, Squaw Grass

Preparation and Uses: Any of the species in

this genus produce edible grain, but the one listed above is probably the best. The hairs on the grain must be singed off before it is used as food.

Mammoth Wild Rye (*E. giganteus*) is sometimes cultivated as an ornamental.

Habitat and Distribution: Wild Rye is found in meadows and on hillsides in moist, often alkaline soils from Montana to Washington, south through Oregon, Idaho, Utah, and Nevada to New Mexico, Arizona, and California.

Description: Wild Rye is a perennial which grows in bunches, usually with broad, flat, blade-like leaves and slender, sometimes dense spikes. The spikelets are 2 - 6 flowered. The glumes are equal, firm, and somewhat asymmetrical. The lemmas are rounded on the back and are awned from the tip, or are awnless.

176. *Avena fatua* and *barbata* (2) (Grass Family)
Wild Oat

Preparation and Uses: The seed is edible, but the hairs must be singed off. The grain can then be ground and used as flour. *A. sativa* is the cultivated oat.

Habitat and Distribution: These plants, introduced from Europe, are widely distributed in open ground throughout the West.

Description: Oats are rather tall and coarse annual grasses. They have relatively broad-bladed leaves and open panicles of large spikelets. The flowers have 2 scales or bracts enclosing them, the larger of which is hairy and both bear a twisted or bent bristle-like appendage.

177. *Sporobolus* species (15) (Grass Family)
Drop Seed

Preparation and Uses: The tiny seeds are relatively easy to harvest since they are fairly free of their husk. They may be eaten raw, but are best when

*Sporobolus
cryptandrus*
Sand Drop Seed

177

176

parched and ground into flour.

Habitat and Distribution: The various species are to be found in diverse habitats from stream side to dry, open ground to alkaline soil throughout the West.

Description: These plants are perennial or annual grasses. The flower stalks vary from a very narrow spike to a quite diffuse panicle. Each spikelet has only one flower.

178. *Oryzopsis hymenoides* and related species
(8) (Grass Family)
Indian Ricegrass, Ricegrass, Mountain Rice

Preparation and Uses: All of the species produce edible seeds that may be eaten raw, but are best when dried and ground into flour for cakes and mush.

Habitat and Distribution: Indian Ricegrass is found in arid regions throughout the West.

Description: The plants are slender, tufted, perennial grasses with many stiff leaf blades whose edges are rolled inward on the upper side. The flowers are in a narrow, spike-like, or open, panicle. Each medium to small sized spikelet has one flower. The glumes are nearly equal.

179. *Eleusine indica* (1) (Grass Family)
Goosegrass

Preparation and Uses: The seeds may be gathered, cleaned, parched, and eaten whole, or ground into flour.

Habitat and Distribution: This introduced grass is found around cultivated areas, and in waste ground in many places in the West.

Description: The plant is a tufted, annual grass with 2 to several stout, one-sided spikes occuring at the end of the stalks. The several-flowered spike-

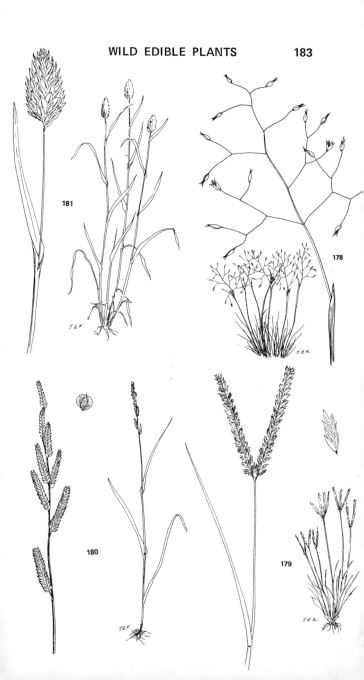

181

178

180

179

lets are flattened in 2 rows. The leaf blades are flat or folded.

180. *Beckmannia syzigachne*
(1) (Grass Family)
Sloughgrass

Preparation and Uses: The seeds were used in pinole by western Indian groups. They may be parched and used whole, or ground into flour.

Habitat and Distribution: As its name indicates, this plant is found in sloughs, ditches, and wet meadows throughout the West.

Description: Sloughgrass is a tall, erect, pale green grass with broad, flat leaves. The flowers are in distended, 2-flowered spikelets, which are arranged in 2 rows along one side of their slender stalk.

181. *Phalaris canariensis*
(1) (Grass Family)
Canary Grass

Preparation and Uses: As its name implies, Canary Grass produced seeds used in canary and other bird seed mixtures. The plant was introduced to the West from the Mediterranean and is found the world over.

The grains measure nearly a quarter of an inch in length and, after thorough cleaning to remove any ergot that might exist, may be used as is any edible grain.

The young, tender plants may be gathered and eaten raw or cooked. They are at their best when mixed with other vegetables or greens.

Habitat and Distribution: Canary Grass may be found growing in occasional waste places throughout the West.

Description: The grass is an erect annual, growing from 1 to 2 feet high. The flowers are borne in broad, dense panicles containing broad, pale, green-striped spikelets.

182. *Digitaria sanguinalis* (1) (Grass Family)
Crab Grass

Preparation and Uses: This common, troublesome weed yields seeds that are rather flavorful when parched and coarsely ground, and eaten as cereal. In northern Europe the seeds are widely used as cereal or finely ground for flour.

Habitat and Distribution: Crab Grass is a common, unwanted weed in lawns, gardens, and fields throughout most of the West.

Description: The grass is an annual, often highly branched at the base, and frequently purplish in color. The ascending flowers are in racemes. The spikelets are in 2's or 3's. Occasionally, however, only one spikelet may appear. The spikelets are quite short, being only 2.5 to 3.5 mm long.

183. *Panicum* species (29) (Grass Family)
Song-wal, Panic Grass

Preparation and Uses: The seeds of the many species are edible raw or ground, and may be used in mush or cakes.

Habitat and Distribution: The various species are found in many habitats throughout the West, frequently in open ground and forest borders. *P. urvilleanum* (Song-Wal), one of the best, is found in the sandy deserts of the Southwest.

Description: These grasses are either annual or perennial and of various habit. The leaves are typically grass-like and are relatively short and broad. Spikelets are flattened and in open or compact panicles or racemes. The glumes are very unequal.

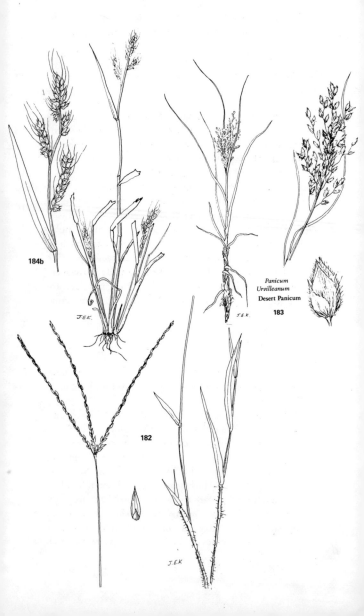

184b

J.E.K.

*Panicum
Urvilleanum*
Desert Panicum
183

J.E.K.

182

J.E.K.

184. *Echinochloa colonum* and *crusgalli*
     (2) (Grass Family)
     Cockspur, Barnyard Grass, Jungle Rice

Preparation and Uses: Both species produce edible seeds, and are today cultivated in Asia and Africa for human food. *E. crusgalli* has been known to absorb toxic amounts of nitrates where fertilizer has been spread on the ground. This is harmful only if the plant is eaten in large quantities.

Habitat and Distribution: These plants are common in moist ground throughout the West.

Description: These are slender or stout annual grasses with flat blades and few to several spikelike racemes along a single axis. The spikelets are bristly and densely arranged along one side of the stem. The first glume is sharp pointed but not tapering and about half as long as the spikelet. The second glume and sterile lemma are equal and pointed.

185. *Setaria* species (8) (Grass Family)
     Foxtail Grass, Bristle Grass, Millet,
     Bristly Foxtail

Preparation and Uses: The seeds should be parched so as to facilitate the removal of the husks. They then may be ground into meal or used whole. In various parts of Europe the seeds are still used in pudding, bread, and soups.

Habitat and Distribution: The Foxtails are found in moist to dry open ground throughout the West.

Description: These annual or perennial grasses have flat leaves. The seeds are in dense, cylindrical spikes, supposedly reminiscent of a fox's tail. Each seed has a long, stiff, bristle on the husk.

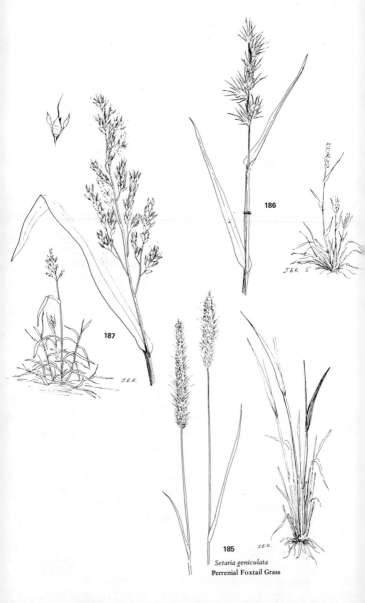

185
Setaria geniculata
Perrenial Foxtail Grass

186. *Cenchrus pauciflorus* and *echinatus*
(2) (Grass Family)
Sandbur, Burgrass

Preparation and Uses: After thorough singeing in open flames to remove the spiny bristles, the seeds may be ground into meal.

Habitat and Distribution: Sandbur is found in sandy or gravelly places throughout the West.

Description: Our 2 western species are low, branching, annual grasses with flat-bladed leaves and split sheaths. The spiny burs develop in simple racemes.

187. *Sorghum halepense* and related species
(3) (Grass Family)
Sorghum, Johnson Grass,
Columbus Grass, Sudan Grass

Preparation and Uses: The seeds may be used in all of the typical ways: meal, mush, parched, ground, etc. The Pima Indians of Arizona used them extensively.

Other sorghums, such as *S. vulgare,* are widely cultivated for agricultural and domestic use. They are divided into saccharin or forage sorghums, grain sorghums, and broom corn. Saccharin or sweet sorghums were once widely used to make syrup but are now mainly grown for forage; they also go under the name of cane sorghums. The grain sorghums are used for both grain and forage. Various names, such as kafir corn, milo, and others are applied to the grain sorghums. Johnson Grass, *S. halepense,* is generally considered a pest in most localities but is cultivated in some places. Some species of this genus have been cultivated in Egypt and other Old World areas for several thousand years.

It is interesting to note that such a widespread and useful plant is not without its dangers. The fresh, green plant contains a compound of cyanide. When used fresh as food for livestock, it can and has caused many cases of cyanide poisoning, resulting in serious livestock loss. When dry, however, the plants are perfectly safe for consumption.

Habitat and Distribution: Sorghums are found in waste places, fields, and along irrigation ditches throughout the West, except, apparently, for most of Washington, Idaho, and Montana.

Description: The sorghums are tall annual or perennial grasses with flat leaf blades and terminal panicles. *S. halepense* has extensive, scaly, heavy rhizomes.

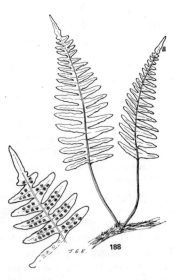

188

PLANTS OF THE NORTHWEST
(Washington, Oregon, and Northwestern California)

These plants, coupled with those found throughout the West, make a fairly extensive list from which to choose edibles. The Northwest is rather varied in climate, topography, and number of available habitats, and this diversity accounts for the fairly large number of edible plants that are particularly characteristic of that region. Some questions may be raised concerning how characteristic of the Northwest some of these plants are, considering that many are also found in the Rocky Mountain region and in California. In some instances the grouping is clear-cut, in others it is not. In fact, because there is a tremendous similarity in plant types between these two regions (and northern California); few of the plants may be classified as unique to the Northwest.

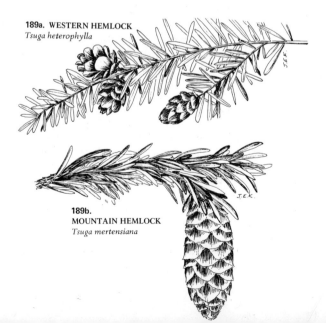

189a. WESTERN HEMLOCK
Tsuga heterophylla

189b.
MOUNTAIN HEMLOCK
Tsuga mertensiana

188.   *Polypodium vulgare* (1) (Fern Division)
       Licorice Fern

   Preparation and Uses: The stem of the leaf, when chewed long enough, develops a distinctive licorice flavor.

   Habitat and Distribution: Licorice Fern is found on moist, shaded, rock ledges, old logs, and mossy trunks of deciduous trees from Alaska southward into California, in the more moist and cool areas.

   Description: This is a typical small fern with firm, creeping rhizomes.   The leaves have jointed stalks, and are pinnately divided in narrow lobes almost reaching the midrib.

189.   *Tsuga heterophylla* and *mertensiana*
       (2) (Pine Family)
       Western Hemlock and Mountain Hemlock

   Preparation and Uses: Western Indians made tea by steeping the fresh needles in hot water for a few minutes.   The inner bark was used in a sort of bread, although it is not particularly flavorful.

   The bark of the Western Hemlock is used today in tanning, and the wood is used for lumber.

   Habitat and Distribution: The hemlocks are forest trees found in Washington, Oregon, and California.

   Description: These are coneshaped, evergreen, coniferous trees with deeply furrowed bark.   The needles are flat or angular, and borne spirally arranged on the twig but appearing 2-ranked to the eye because of twisting by the needle.

190.   *Dentaria* species (4) (Mustard Family)
       Toothwort, Pepperroot, Dentaria

   Preparation and Uses: The crispy rootstock may be eaten raw and is good in salads.

Habitat and Distribution: The various species are found on shady banks, rocky slopes, and in moist places, generally in mountain and coastal areas of the Pacific Coast states.

Description: The Toothworts are perennials rising from thick, fleshy, stout rootstocks or tubers. The stems are erect, nearly hairless, usually unbranched, leafless below, with a few leaves on the upper stem. The leaves are basal, rising directly from the rootstock. The white to rose or purple flowers are borne in a raceme.

191. *Thysanocarpus curvipes* (1) (Mustard Family)
Lacepod, Fringe Pod

Preparation and Uses: The seeds may be parched and eaten or ground into flour.

Habitat and Distribution: Lacepod is common on grassy to brushy slopes, and in dry, sandy areas on both sides of the Cascade Mountains in Washington, on south into California, on the coast, and east into Idaho.

Description: This plant is a slender, erect annual with purplish flowers. The oblong, basal leaves are coarsely toothed. The small stem leaves are mostly entire. The pendulous seed pods are quite flattened and bear a fringe resembling lace.

192. *Calandrinia ciliata* and related species
(4) (Purslane Family)
Red Maids, Rose Calandrinia

Preparation and Uses: All of the species are edible raw or cooked. The seeds may be eaten raw or ground into meal.

Habitat and Distribution: Red Maids are found in moist to dry, open or shaded ground in the Pacific states and Arizona.

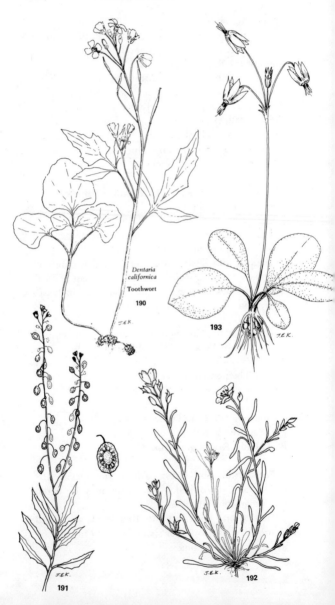

*Dentaria
californica*
Toothwort
190

191

192

193

Description: Our native *Calandrinia* are somewhat fleshy, annual herbs with alternate, entire leaves. The red, rarely white, short-lived flowers have 3 to 7 petals, 2 sepals, a 3-cleft style, and are borne in leafy racemes or panicles. The numerous, rounded, very dark seeds are flattened.

193. *Dodecatheon hendersonii* (1) (Primrose Family)
Shooting Star, Henderson's Shooting Star,
Broad-leaved Shooting Star

Preparation and Uses: The roots and leaves may be eaten roasted or boiled. Since none of the species are listed anywhere as poisonous it is likely, but unknown for sure, that all are edible.

Habitat and Distribution: Shooting Star is found in dry, open woods west of the Cascades from Washington into California.

Description: This shooting star is a hairless plant rising with a very short caudex from fleshy, fibrous roots. The round to oval leaves are 1 to 3 inches long and have petioles as long or longer than the leaves. The 4 to 16 inch high flower stem bears an umbel composed of 3 to 10 rose to rose-purple flowers, each with a basal zone of black, and an upper zone of yellow.

194. *Gaultheria shallon* and *ovatifolia*
(2) (Heath Family)
Salal

Preparation and Uses: The thick skinned berries are tasty raw or cooked.

Habitat and Distribution: *G. shallon* is found in woods and clearings along the coast from British Columbia to California and east to the west slope of the Cascades. Distribution of *G. ovatifolia* is the same except that it grows further east to Idaho and the Blue Mountains of Oregon.

Description: *G. shallon* is a rigid, freely branched shrub 1-8 feet high, sometimes forming impenetrable thickets. The leaves are oblong to elliptic, narrowed at the apex, broadest near the base, minutely toothed, dark green, shiny on top, paler green underneath, 1½ to 4 inches long. The racemes are terminal on the branches and 5-15 flowered; the flowers all lean to one side. The flower peduncles all bear a white or reddish bract and two bractlets at their bases. The flower is white or pinkish, the fruit black.

G. ovatifolia is similar to the above, but is a slender, prostrate shrub with spreading branches. It reaches 2-6 inches in height. The leaves are thick, narrowing at the apex, broadest and rounded near the base. The flowers are white, bell-shaped and solitary. The fruit is red.

195. *Arbutus menziesii* and *arizonica*
      (2) (Heath Family)
      Madrone

Preparation and Uses: The scarlet berries may be eaten raw, boiled, or steamed. After boiling they may be dried for future use; they keep well dried.

Habitat and Distribution: This tree is found at lower elevations in the mountains from western British Columbia south into California.

Description: Madrone are trees or shrubs with smooth, thin bark which peels off in layers, and is sometimes somewhat fissured on the main trunk. The leaves are evergreen, thick, shiny, and arranged alternately. The scarlet fruit is berrylike with a rough surface.

196. *Empetrum nigrum* (1) (Crowberry Family)
      Crowberry

Preparation and Uses: The black berries may be

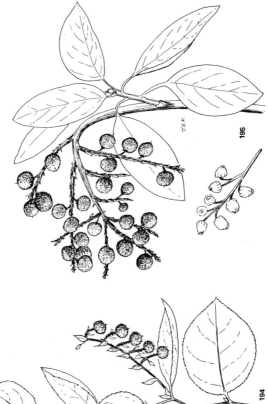

eaten raw or cooked, and are quite juicy. To some the flavor is slightly disagreeable but it is a flavor that grows on one. The taste is improved if the berries are cooked and sugar added before eating. The berries are also good in puddings, muffins, and pancakes.

The berries are sometimes used to make a sort of beer by crushing them, adding sugar, brown sugar, or molasses, putting them in an air tight container and allowing them to ferment for a few days. The resultant liquid is then strained, cooled, and drunk. Wine may also be made from the berries.

Habitat and Distribution: Crowberry is found forming dense mats in rocky places on coastal sea bluffs from northwestern California to Alaska.

Description: Crowberry is a prostrate, spreading, heathlike, highly branched shrub, with many small, rigid, narrow, dark-green leaves with rolled under margins. The small, inconspicuous flowers are purplish in color. The berries are black.

197. *Satureja douglasii* (1) (Mint Family)
Yerba Buena, Oregon Tea

Preparation and Uses: The dry leaves may be steeped for fifteen to twenty minutes in hot water to make a good tea said to be stimulating to the digestion.

Habitat and Distribution: Yerba Buena is found in open woods from British Columbia south into California.

Description: This plant is a perennial with a slender, creeping, woody stem ½ to 3 inches long. The opposite leaves are ovate, ½ to 1½ inches long and are either smooth or clothed with very fine short hairs. The white flowers are solitary in the axils of the leaves.

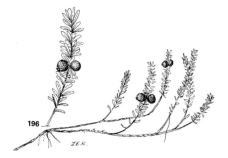

196

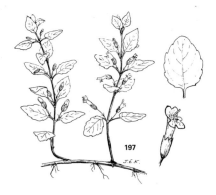

197

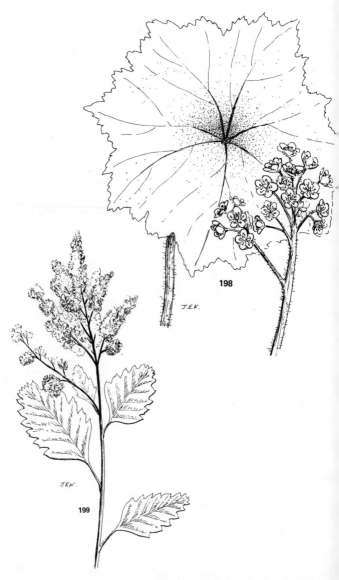

198

J.E.K.

J.E.K.

199

198. *Peltiphyllum peltatum* (1) (Saxifrage Family)
Indian Rhubarb, Great Shieldleaf

Preparation and Uses: The fleshy leafstalks may be peeled and eaten as is, or in salad. They may also be added to stews, or used alone as a potherb, but cooking destroys some of their flavor.

Habitat and Distribution: Indian Rhubarb is found on banks and rocks of mountain streams and rivers, often with its thick rhizome well exposed, in the Sierra Nevada from Tulare County, California, north to Humboldt and Siskiyou Counties, and on into southern Oregon.

Description: The plant is a coarse perennial herb with large roundish leaves whose thick, fleshy stalks attach to the middle underside of the leaf. All of the leaves rise from a thick rhizome. The small, 5-petaled, white to pink flowers are borne in a cyme.

199. *Holodiscus discolor* (1) (Rose Family)
Mountainspray, Ocean Spray, Creambush, Foambush, Rock-Spirea

Preparation and Uses: The one-seeded fruits were eaten raw or cooked by many western Indians.

Habitat and Distribution: This plant is found in woods, rocky places, and along stream banks in western Montana, Idaho, Washington, Oregon, and California.

Description: Mountainspray is a spreading, much branched shrub growing 4 to 18 feet tall with oval, toothed to lobed leaves that are hairy on the underneath side. The twigs are straw-colored, while older bark varies from brownish or gray to dark red. The creamy-white flowers occur in large, dense masses. The small, dry, hard, 1-seeded fruits have a straight upper edge, and a convex lower edge.

200. *Osmaronia cerasiformis* (1) (Rose Family)
Oso Berry, Indian Plum

Preparation and Uses: The berry is rather disagreeably flavored, but nevertheless it is quite edible raw or cooked.

Habitat and Distribution: Oso Berry is found in thickets west of the Cascade Mountains from British Columbia south to central California.

Description: The plant is a shrub with simple, entire, oblong leaves, and smooth, gray to red-brown bark. The leaves are paler beneath than above, and somewhat hairy beneath.

201. *Malus fusca* (1) (Rose Family)
Oregon Crab Apple

Preparation and Uses: The small apples of this native tree may be eaten raw and make good jelly, pies, applesauce, etc. Occasionally one sees the common, introduced, commercial apple, *M. sylvestris,* escaped from cultivation, or maintaining itself on old, abandoned farmsteads.

It should be noted that all apples have seeds that are high in cyanide content. Human deaths have been recorded from eating too many apple-seeds.

Habitat and Distribution: The Oregon Crab Apple is found in woods and thickets near the coast in Sonoma and Napa counties in west-central California, northward through Oregon and Washington west of the Cascades, to Alaska.

Description: The plant is a large shrub to small tree, reaching 30 feet or more in height. The alternate, oval, toothed leaves are sometimes lobed. The white flowers occur in small, rather flattopped clusters. The fruit is a typical apple, although oval in shape.

202. *Cytisus scoparius* (1) (Pea Family)
Scotch Broom

Preparation and Uses: The roasted seeds may be used as a substitute for coffee. The lower buds and pods can be made into good pickles by putting them into a very heavy brine of white-wine vinegar and salt, weighting them to hold them under the brine. After soaking in this solution overnight, remove the buds and pods, rinse them, and put them up in any good pickle solution that you like, weight them under again and leave until they will not float, after which they may be used any time.

The fresh buds and pods should not be eaten, for they, like the foliage, contain small amounts of toxic alkaloids.

Habitat and Distribution: Although this plant is a native of Europe, it has become widely established over thousands of acres in the 3 western coastal states, and is common on roadsides and slopes.

Description: Scotch Broom is a highly branched, large shrub growing to 10 feet in height in a moist habitat. The leaves are well developed only on young plants; the branchlets are deep green and sometimes spiny. The bright-yellow, showy, pea-like flowers are very abundant, and are borne 1 or 2 to 3 to an axil. The brownish-black seed pods are shaggily hairy on the margins.

203. *Lathyrus japonicus* (1) (Pea Family)
Beach-Pea, Purple Beach-Pea

Preparation and Uses: The young pods and seeds are sweet and good eaten raw. When mature they are best boiled in soup.

Although this species has never been found to be toxic, a number of other species of this genus have. Evidently these plants have a history of poisoning humans dating back to Grecian times. There have

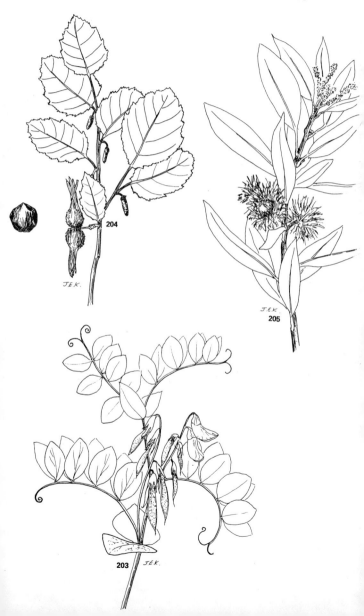

been epidemics of lathyrism reported, usually associated with conditions of drought or poverty which encourage people to increase the amount of these plants in their diet. Eaten daily in normal amount, many of these plants are nutritious food. During periods of starvation, an almost exclusive diet of some species will, after ten days to four weeks, bring on partial or total paralysis in humans. A variety of secondary disorders accompany the paralysis, but are lost if the diet is corrected. The paralysis, however, is permanent. Even the common garden pea *(Pisum)*, closely related to *Lathyrus* can cause nervous disorders if eaten in great quantities over long periods of time.

Habitat and Distribution: The Beach-Pea is found on, or close to, the ocean beaches from Alaska to California.

Description: The stems are smooth, rather stout, at first erect and then reclining or prostrate, and pale green in color. Leaflets number 6-12 and are in pairs, are elliptic or ovate and 1-2 inches long. The stipules are as large as the leaflets and are sharply pointed. The fairly long peduncles support 6 to 10 purple flowers.

204. *Corylus cornuta* (1) (Birch Family)
      Beaked Hazelnut, Western Hazel, Hazelnut

Preparation and Uses: The sweet nuts ripen from August to October, and are similar to ordinary commercial hazelnuts (filberts). They are delicous when ground into meal and made into bread.

Habitat and Distribution: The Hazelnut is found in woods and thickets mainly west of the Cascade Mountains of Oregon, north to British Columbia, and south into California.

Description: The Beaked Hazelnut is an open, spreading, smooth-barked shrub or small tree reaching 20 feet in height. The rounded, doubly toothed, sometimes lobed leaves are pale beneath. The nuts are contained within very bristly husks.

205a. *Castanopsis chrysophylla* (1) (Beech Family)
Chinquapin

205b. *Castanopsis sempervirens* (1)
Bush Chinquapin

Preparation and Uses: The nuts of these species ripen in September and are sweet and pleasant to the taste. They are also excellent when roasted in the ashes of a campfire.

Habitat and Distribution: The Chinquapin is found in open woods at low elevations in the Cascades of Washington and Oregon, and the South Coast Range in Oregon and northern California.

Description: They are evergreen shrubs or trees. The leaves are simple. Staminate flowers are in threes along the elongate catkins. The calyx is 5-6 parted. Stamens number 6-17. Pistillate flowers number 1-3. Here the calyx is 6-cleft with vestigial stamens. Nuts number 1-3 in a cluster and are each encased in a spiny bur.

206. *Myrica gale* (1) (Walnut Family)
Sweet Gale

Preparation and Uses: The leaves have a pungent, spicy odor and, when dried, make an excellent seasoning with meat. The leaves also make a good tea. The nutlets may be used as a spice.

Habitat and Distribution: Sweet Gale is found in sphagnum bogs along the coast of Oregon, Washington, and British Columbia to Alaska.

Description: Sweet Gale is a much-branched shrub growing from 1 to 5 feet high. The leaves are narrowly obovate, grayish-green, and yellow-dotted with resin, especially beneath. The top

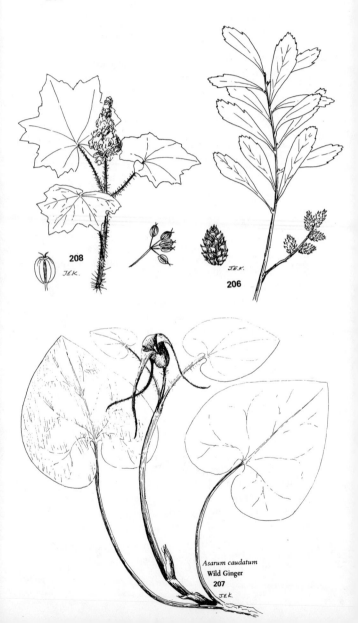

Asarum caudatum
Wild Ginger
207

half of the leaf is toothed, while the bottom half is entire.

207. *Asarum* species (3) (Birthwort Family)
Wild Ginger, Ginger

Preparation and Uses: Any of the species have a rootstock that may be used as a substitute for commercial ginger. It may be dried for storage, or candied by cutting it into short pieces, boiling in water until tender, and then boiling the pieces in a heavy syrup.

Habitat and Distribution: Wild Ginger is found in cool, moist, shady ground in Washington, Idaho, Oregon, and California.

Description: Wild Ginger is a stemless, perennial herb rising from a branching rootstock. The few leaves are basal, large, long-petioled, more or less oval-arrowhead-shaped, and aromatic. The large flowers are solitary.

208. *Oplopanax horridum*
(1) (Ginsing Family)
Devil's Club

Preparation and Uses: The young stems may be eaten cooked as greens. The roots may be peeled and chewed.

Habitat and Distribution: Devil's Club is found along damp stream banks in the mountains of Oregon on north to Alaska.

Description: This is a stout, shrubby plant with stems densely covered by long, yellowish prickels. The large, petioled, simple, roundish, deeply lobed leaves have prickly veins. The greenish flowers develop into scarlet fruit.

209. *Cornus nuttallii* (Dogwood Family)
(Western Flowering Dogwood)

209

210

211

Preparation and Uses. The inner bark of twigs was scraped off and used to add to tobacco for smoking; leaves sometimes used; both dried or roasted. The berries were sometimes eaten raw or cooked. Refer to *C. canadensis* in the West.

Habitat and Distribution: Found in mixed woods or along streams at moderate elevations from British Columbia south, west of the Cascades to California.

Description: 10 to 45 foot high tree, with quite smooth bark; what look like very large white-petaled flowers are actually flower heads surrounded by conspicuous flower bracts; berries are scarlet.

210. *Inula helenium* (1) (Sunflower Family)
Elecampane

Preparation and Uses: The young, bitter leaves may be boiled and eaten, and were so used by the Romans. The cooked, candied roots make a pleasing confection. The root has been considered a sort of cure-all for two thousand years or more in southern Europe. Pliny, for example, writes that the roots will aid digestion and improve your disposition.

Habitat and Distribution: This plant is found in open ground west of the Cascades from Washington to northwestern California. It was introduced as a garden plant from Europe and is not common.

Description: Elecampane is a tall, coarse perennial with alternate, simple, basal leaves, and large yellow flower heads. The leaves are densely hairy on the underneath side.

211. *Zostera marina* (1) (Eel Grass Family)
Eel Grass

Preparation and Uses: The rootstocks and bases of the shoots may be chewed raw for their sweetish juice. The chewed material should be discarded, however, since it is hard to digest.

Description: This is one of the few marine flowering plants. It grows submerged from creeping rootstocks, and produces long, narrow, bright-green leaves with 3 to 5 distinct nerves. The sexes are separate, with male and female flowers alternating in 2 rows on a one-sided spike.

Habitat and Distribution: Eel Grass is found in the shallow water of coastal pools and bays from San Diego to Alaska.

212.   *Xerophyllum tenax* (1) (Lily Family)
Bear Grass, Indian Basket Grass, Pine Lily

Preparation and Uses: The fibrous root is best eaten when roasted or boiled. Indians once used the leaves for making clothing and decorating baskets.

Habitat and Distribution: Bear Grass is found on open slopes in the mountains of Washington, Oregon, Idaho, California, Wyoming, and Montana.

Description: This member of the lily family grows 2-3 feet high and bears a large head of white flowers. The stem is thickly covered with needle-like leaves; those near the bottom are quite long and become shorter toward the flower head where they are almost reduced to bracts.

213.   *Camassia* species (5) (Lily Family)
Camas, Blue Camas

Preparation and Uses: The several species all have edible bulbs which may be eaten raw but are at their best when cooked. For the finest flavor, the Indian method of steaming in a fire pit is best. Ten or more pounds of bulbs are placed in the fire pit (see *glossary*) for at least twenty-four hours. At the end of this time the cooked mass will be dark brown in color, soft and sweet to the taste. It may be eaten immediately, or pressed into cakes and dried over a fire or in the sun.

Habitat and Distribution: Camas are most com-

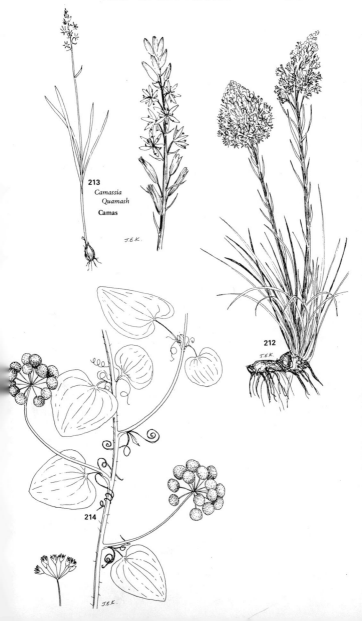

213
Camassia
Quamash
Camas

J.E.K.

212
J.E.K.

214

J.E.K.

monly found in moist meadows of the forested valleys and mountains of Washington and Oregon, but two species occur in California and one in western Nevada.

Description: Camas are herbaceous plants with flowers 1-2 inches in diameter arranged in a simple raceme. The flowers are commonly blue, but white is not rare. The leaves are slender, several and basal. Sepals and petals together number 6 and are separate. Stamens number 6. The style is 3-cleft at the apex.

The Death-camas *(Zygadenus spp.)*, with its cream-colored flowers is often found growing among edible blue Camas. The plant is a common source of poisoning and death in livestock, but most human cases date from the years when the West was being settled. Although both Indians and settlers were aware of this toxic plant, they occasionally ate the wrong bulbs by mistake. Probably the only safe way to eat Camas is to collect the bulbs of the blue flowered specimens to be sure of excluding the Death camas.

214. *Smilax californica* (1) (Lily Family)
Greenbrier

Preparation and Uses: The roots may be used in soups and stews, or dried and ground into flour. The dried roots may also be chopped and boiled with sugar to make jelly. The flour, mixed with water and sweetened with sugar, or preferably, honey, makes an excellent drink. By itself, the flour and water mixture resembles sarsaparilla, which is not surprising since the sarsaparilla of commerce is a tropical species, *S. officinalis,* of this genus.

The young, vigorously growing, spring shoots may be eaten raw or cooked.

Habitat and Distribution: Greenbrier is found

along stream banks and in thickets where there is sufficient moisture, from the Rogue River Valley of southern Oregon to Napa County in California.

Description: Our western Greenbrier has rather woody, frequently climbing stems, 3 to 10 feet long, that are often slightly prickly. The heart-shaped, sharp-pointed leaves are thin and hairless. The greenish flowers are borne in umbels.

215. *Lysichiton americanum* (1) (Arum Family)
Yellow Skunk Cabbage, Skunk Cabbage

Preparation and Uses: The root becomes edible after roasting and drying, and may be ground into a starchy flour. The young green leaves may be eaten after being boiled in several waters. Calcium oxalate is found throughout the plant and if not roasted or boiled sufficiently, a choking sensation, often accompanied by a burning in the mouth and throat, may occur.

It is interesting to note that Skunk Cabbage is related to that Polynesian staple, Taro, which also contains calcium oxalate. It, too, must be cooked to remove the noxious compound.

Habitat and Distribution: Skunk Cabbage is found in open swamps and very wet woods from northern California to Alaska, and east to western Montana at low elevations.

Description: This plant is a large, herbaceous perennial with a fleshy rootstock, and large, oblong, basal leaves. The numerous, yellowish flowers are borne on a stout, fleshy, central stem. A large, yellow, malodorous (the inspiration, no doubt, for the name of Skunk Cabbage) leaf partly surrounds the flower stalk.

216. *Zizania aquatica* (1) (Grass Family)
Wildrice

Preparation and Uses: The grains may be used in the same way as ordinary rice, to which it is much superior in flavor.

Habitat and Distribution: Wildrice, a native of the Great Lakes area, has been introduced to Colorado but apparently has not persisted there. It is occasionally found in marshes and shallow water in Idaho.

Description: Wildrice is a broad-leaved grass of semi-aquatic habitat, and bears large terminal panicles. The lower branches of the plant are somewhat spreading.

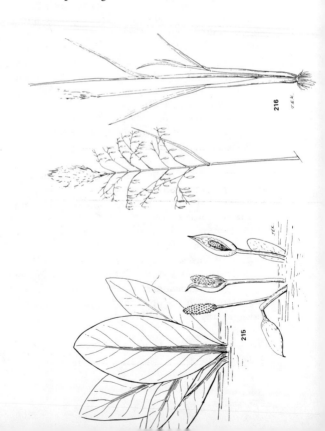

PLANTS OF THE SOUTHWEST

It is interesting to note that, except for the plants found throughout the West, this geographical area has the largest number of edible plants. One reason for this is that the climate of the Southwest is more diverse than that of the Northwest or the Rockies.

Another possible reason is that many of the Indians of the Southwest were agriculturists to a greater or lesser degree. Farming allowed them a certain amount of leisure time as is evidenced by the elaborate ceremonial rituals that have developed in the Southwest. Having some leisure time, they were probably motivated to experiment with native plants to see which were edible and worth cultivating. As a matter of fact, a number of native plants listed in this chapter, such as the tepary bean *(Phaseolus acutifolius)*, were once grown by various Indian tribes, and some are still being cultivated.

Although the corn plant is native to America, it is not included in this list. Corn as we know it will not grow wild, but requires a certain amount of care. Furthermore, it is strongly felt that this highly domesticated plant originated somewhere in southern Mexico and is the hybrid of several other plants.

217. *Pellaea mucronata* (1) (Fern Division)
      Bird's Foot Fern, Tea Fern, Cliff Brake

   Preparation and Uses: The dried fronds may be
steeped in hot water for 15 to 20 minutes to produce a fragrant and flavorful tea. In pioneer days an
extra strong brew of the tea was used in treating
tuberculosis and feverish colds. In making such tea
the entire plant was used.
   Habitat and Distribution: Bird's Foot Fern is
found on dry, rocky slopes nearly throughout inter-
mountain California, but sparingly on the desert.
   Description: This fern has a thick, woody rhizome covered with tufted, dark-brown scales. The
divisions of the leaves resemble the arrangement of
a bird's foot, hence the common name. The fern
above ground is a gray-green color.

218. *Pinus edulis, monophylla, quadrifolia*
      and related species (21) (Pine Family)
      Pinon Pine, Nut Pine, Pine

   Preparation and Uses: Many of the species of
this genus produce delicious nuts, but the three
named above are the best. The nuts may be found
in late August and September within the cone and
removed just before ripe by roasting the cone. An
easier method, if there are not too many squirrels
in the area, is simply to gather them from the
ground where they have fallen after the cone has
opened. Sometimes one is able to rob a rodent's
nest of his often large supply of nuts. The nuts are
thin shelled, from ½ to ¾ of an inch long, and
rather tedious to crack. However, they are flavorful, nutritious, and easily digested.
   The nuts were widely used by Indians who mashed them up, shell and all. These trees are today the
objects of great abuse by people who, with chain-
saws, cut down entire trees to harvest the green

217

219

218

nut-filled cones.

Habitat and Distribution: The Pinon Pines are natives of our greater Southwest, inhabiting slopes and canyons just above the sagebrush desert. The pines as a group are spread throughout the West.

Description: Pines are evergreen trees, the Pinons being rather spreading in growth form. The needles are borne in clusters as opposed to singly in fir trees. *P. monophylla,* the Single-leaved Pinon, does have most of its needles borne singly, however. A Pinon Pine cone takes two years to mature so a large crop of nuts usually occurs only every other year.

219. *Umbellularia californica* (1) (Laurel Family)
California Laurel, California Bay, Myrtle,
Oregon Myrtle

Preparation and Uses: The thin-shelled nuts may be parched and eaten, or ground into flour and baked as bread. An infusion of the leaves can be used as a disinfectant. The wood is hard, strong and takes a high polish. It is prized for the manufacture of small wood turnings such as bowls, platters, candlesticks, etc., and as such goes under the name of Oregon Myrtle, or Myrtlewood.

Habitat and Distribution: The plant is found in woods and thickets from southwestern Oregon to southern California.

Description: California Laurel is an evergreen, aromatic shrub or small tree with leathery, simple, alternate, oblong-lanceolate leaves that often show a number of colored dots interrupting their smooth green color. The yellow-green flowers develop into a brown-stoned, purple fruit.

220. *Malvastrum exile* (1) (Mallow Family)
White Mallow

Preparation and Uses: The entire plant above ground is edible, but is one of those that is not particularly palatable. It was used by the Pima Indians of Arizona in time of scarcity.

Habitat and Distribution: The plant is common in dry, open places from southwestern Utah to southern Arizona and California.

Description: *M. exile* is a prostrate, herbaceous annual with several 4 to 16 inch stems rising from the base. The roundish leaves are palmately 3 to 5 cleft. The flowers are pale lavender to white or sometimes pink.

221. *Croton corymbulosus* (1) (Spurge Family)
Chaparral Tea

Preparation and Uses: A tea may be made by steeping the flowering tips in hot water. *C. texensis* and *C. capitatus* are listed in Kingsbury as sometimes poisonous to livestock. *C. tiglium* is the source of croton oil, once used in medicine as an extremely strong purgative. Kingsbury notes that only a few drops of the pure oil are lethal to animals.

Habitat and Distribution: Chaparral Tea is common on dry, rocky slopes from Texas to southern Arizona and New Mexico.

Description: Chaparral Tea is a shrubby perennial herb with simple, petioled, alternate leaves. The flowers are borne in racemes.

222. *Fouquieria splendens* (1) (Ocotillo Family)
Ocotillo, Coach-whip, Slimwood

Preparation and Uses: The capsules and flowers may be eaten raw or cooked. This interesting plant is often used as a living fence. Cuttings root readily and may be simply stuck in the soil to root. The Ocotillo drops its leaves soon after the soil dries

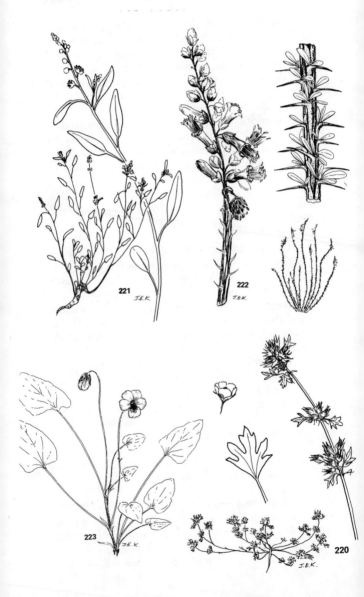

but quickly refoliates after a good rain. An excellent leather dressing can be made from the wax coating found on the stems. The powdered roots are reported to be helpful when applied to painful swellings and to relieve fatigue when added to a bath.

Habitat and Distribution: Ocotillo are found on dry desert mesas and slopes from western Texas to southeastern California and northern Mexico.

Description: The Ocotillo is a quite distinctive, large, thorny shrub with many long whiplike, un-branched stems covered with green bark. The leaves when present, are light green and small. The flowers are showy, and bright red at the ends of the stems. The plant may reach fifteen feet in height.

223. *Viola pedunculata* (1) (Violet Family)
Pansy Violet, Violet, Johnny-Jump-Up,
Wild Pansy

Preparation and Uses: The leaves and stems are good when eaten as greens.

Habitat and Distribution: The Johnny-Jump-Up is a California plant found on dry, grassy or brushy slopes below 7000 feet in the foothills surrounding the Central Valley, and in the inner Coast Ranges from San Diego to southern Oregon.

Description: This violet is a perennial with several slender stems rising from thick, fleshy roots. The branching, minutely hairy stems are prostrate but with the tips curving upward. The bright green, rather oval-shaped leaves have coarse, rounded teeth on the margin. The orange-yellow flowers have 2 upper petals that are red-brown on the back, and 3 lower ones that have dark brown veins.

224. *Wislizenia refracta* (1) (Caper Family)
Jackass Clover

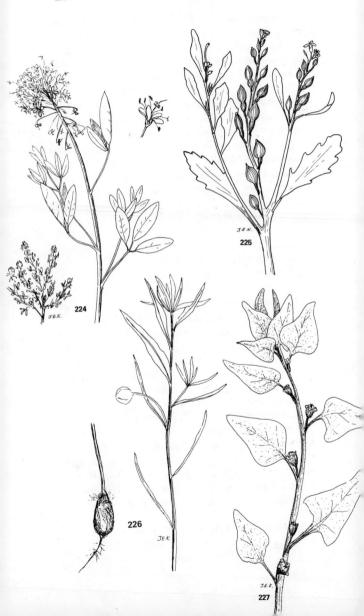

Preparation and Uses: The plant may be used as a potherb.

Habitat and Distribution: Jackass Clover is found in sandy, often rather alkaline, soil from western Texas across to southern California.

Description: This is an erect, highly-branched, annual herb bearing mostly trifoliate leaves. The yellow, small, numerous flowers are in a raceme, and have 4 petals, 4 sepals, and 6 stamens.

225. *Cakile edentula* (1) (Mustard Family)
Sea Rocket

Preparation and Uses: The young leaves and shoots, although strongly flavored, are edible raw, and are good in salads. Cooking is a must for older plants and much improves the flavor of young plants.

Habitat and Distribution: Sea Rocket is found in beach sands from San Diego to British Columbia.

Description: Sea Rocket is a hairless, fleshy, succulent annual with wavy margined, rather wedge-shaped leaves. The purplish to white flowers have 2 pairs of opposite petals. The seeds are borne in plump pods.

226. *Talinum aurantiacum* (1) (Purslane Family)
Fame Flower

Preparation and Uses: The roots may be cooked and eaten, although when large they tend to become woody.

Habitat and Distribution: Fame Flower is found on plains and rocky slopes, often among grasses, in southern New Mexico, southern Arizona, and northern Mexico.

Description: This is a hairless, perennial herb rising from bulbous rootstocks, and bearing narrow, alternate, leaves. The orange or copper-colored flowers are solitary, or in few-flowered cymes.

227. *Tetragonia expansa* (1) (Carpet-Weed Family)
New Zealand Spinach

Preparation and Uses: This succulent herb may be cooked in the same way as spinach.

Habitat and Distribution: The plant, a native of southeast Asia, has become established near salt marshes, and on beaches all along the California and Oregon coasts.

Description: This is a spreading, succulent annual containing many small, crystalline cavities. The triangular to oval leaves are entire to wavy margined. The yellow-green, solitary flowers are located in axils and have spreading sepals.

228. *Mesembryanthemum crystallinum* and *edule*
(2) (Carpet-Weed Family)
Ice Plant, Sea Fig, Hottentot Fig

Preparation and Uses: Both of these plants, the Ice Plant or Sea Fig, and the Hottentot Fig, were introduced to California from Africa and have become widespread. The leaves and stems are quite fleshy and may be used in salads. When cooked, much of their appeal is lost. The fruit is also edible.

Habitat and Distribution: These two species are much planted along the coast and along highways and banks to reduce erosion. They have, as a result, become widely naturalized in coastal dunes.

Description: The plants are low growing, fleshy herbs. The flowers are many-petaled. The leaves of *M. crystallinum* are oval to spatula-shaped, while those of *M. edule* are narrow and distinctly 3-sided. The magenta flowers of *M. edule* are quite showy. The flowers of *M. crystallinum* are white to reddish.

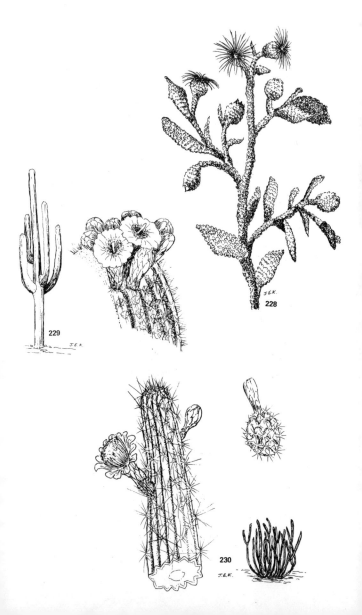

229. *Cereus (Carnegiea) giganteus* (1) (Cactus Family)
Saguaro, Sahuaro, Giant Cactus

Preparation and Uses: The crimson red, juicy pulp of the fruit is edible raw, or it can be boiled until the seeds are easily removed, then boiled down further to make an excellent syrup. The sweet syrup is a clear, light brown color and may be used in making preserves.

A sort of wine can be made by allowing the juice of the fresh fruit to ferment. The raw fruit may be peeled and the inner pulp dried for future use. The oily seeds may be mashed into a paste and used like butter.

Habitat and Distribution: Saguaro is found in well drained desert soil in southern Arizona and in a small area in southeastern California near the Colorado River.

Description: This is the largest United States cactus, being tree-like in size and growth habit, and occasionally reaching 50 feet in height. The massive, continuous, columnar trunk usually bears several erect branches well above the ground. The stout, many-ribbed trunk is heavily covered with stiff, straight spines. The white, spineless, funnel-shaped flowers are night-blooming. The fruit is oblong.

230. *Lemaireocereus thurberi* (1) (Cactus Family)
Organpipe Cactus

Preparation and Uses: The large spiny fruits can be used in the same manner as the Saguaro.

Habitat and Distribution: Organpipe Cactus is found in southern Arizona, southern Sonora, and Baja California.

Description: This cactus is quite large, almost tree-like, with many branches rising from the base. The spiny, many-ribbed stems bear pink, funnel-shaped, night-blooming flowers. The globe-shaped fruit is quite spiny.

231. *Echinocactus* species (8) (Cactus Family)
Barrel Cactus, Bisnaga, Devil's Head Cactus

Preparation and Uses: When one thinks of a thirsty desert traveler, this plant usually comes to mind, although it was used more often for food than for a water supply. The popular view of this famous cactus is that of a hollow, spiny covered water barrel, and that the traveler need only cut off the top to dip out a gallon or so of cool, clear liquid. Such is not the case. The Barrel Cactus can indeed supply a good quantity of water, depending on its size, but the water must be squeezed from the pulp hidden behind the tough thorny rind.

For food preparation, the thorny skin should be peeled away, and the pulp left in position for a few days to "bleed." Then cut the pulp into small pieces and boil in saguaro syrup or sweetened water. It is then ready to eat. Today the flesh of many of these cacti, cooked in sugar, is an ingredient for cactus candy.

Habitat and Distribution: *Echinocactus* species are found in desert areas throughout the southwest into Mexico.

Description: The various species range from 2 to 10 feet in height. The simple stems are cylindric, ribbed and armed with stout, often hooked spines. The flowers are more or less in the shape of a funnel and range in color from yellow to orange and rose-pink, forming a ring around the crown of the cactus.

232. *Peniocereus greggii* (1) (Cactus Family)
Night-blooming Cereus, Reina de la Noche,
Deerhorn Cactus

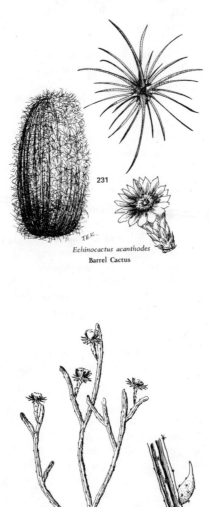

Echinocactus acanthodes
Barrel Cactus

Preparation and Uses: The large root may be baked or boiled and eaten, or used in other ways. It commonly weighs from 5 to 15 pounds, but specimens of 85 to 87 pounds have been recorded.

Habitat and Distribution: This plant is found among Creosote Bushes from western Texas through southern New Mexico, to Arizona and northern Mexico.

Description: The plant commonly grows 1 to 5 feet tall with slender stems rising from the large beet-like root. The strongly angled stems have a few prominent ribs and are densely covered with fine soft hairs. The sparse spines are short and dark. The large white flowers bloom at night.

233. *Eriogonum inflatum* and related species
(121) (Buckwheat Family)
Desert Trumpet, Wild Buckwheat

Preparation and Uses: Many of the species are worth eating and none are known to be poisonous. The stems may be eaten raw or cooked before they have flowered.

Habitat and Distribution: The plants are found in desert areas on many hills from Utah and Arizona to southern California and Baja California. It also is found on dry hills and plains from southern Colorado through New Mexico into Mexico.

Description: This genus includes annuals and perennials, herbs and shrubs. The leaves are alternate or whorled, entire and simple. The larger leaves often form a basal rosette. Bract-like leaves often occur on the stem. The flowers are small and number several to many. The stamens number 9.

234. *Acanthochiton wrightii* (1) (Amaranth Family)
(No common name) (Illustration not shown)

Preparation and Uses: The entire plant above

ground is edible as a green, or it can be dried and stored for future use.

Habitat and Distribution: This plant is found in desert areas from western Texas to Arizona and Chihuahua.

Description: *Acanthochiton wrightii* is an annual with smooth, hairless, branched, erect stems which are striped green and white. The sexes are commonly separate; pistillate flowers being found on one plant and staminate on another. The staminate flowers are in small heads or head-like divisions or formations, which, taken together, form spikes with a bractless, 5-segmented perianth (calyx and corolla, usually when they are similar). The pistillate flowers have no perianth, and are subtended (under or supporting) by heart-shaped bracts (reduced or modified leaves) which become spiny with age.

235. *Phytolacca americana* (1) (Pokeweed Family) Pokeberry, Pokeweed, Pigeon Berry

Preparation and Uses: The roots are quite poisonous and must be avoided, but the young shoots about 6 inches high or under make an excellent potherb.

The berries are reported by some to be edible and by others to be poisonous. Those that use them make them into pies and jellies. The concentrated purple juice has been used as a food coloring. This is one native plant that has been widely established in gardens in southern Europe.

Habitat and Distribution: Pokeberry is found in open ground from Texas across New Mexico and Arizona to southern California and northward to Siskiyou County, California.

Description: Pokeberry is a tall, stout, perennial herb rising from a large, fleshy taproot. The large,

233

235

alternate, petioled leaves are oblong to lanceolate. The stems are smooth, hairless, purple or green, and grow to 9 feet in height. The small, white or greenish flowers are in a terminal raceme which droops with the weight of the fruit.

236. *Sarcostemma* species (4) (Milkweed Family) Climbing Milkweed

Preparation and Uses: The fruits may be eaten raw or cooked.

Habitat and Distribution: These plants are found from western Texas to southern Nevada, southeastern California and on south to Mexico.

Description: The Climbing Milkweeds are twining or trailing vines bearing numerous, opposite, triangular to oval leaves with heart-shaped bases. The fragrant, white, yellow or purplish, numerous flowers are borne in lateral umbels. The club-shaped to spindle-shaped, dry fruits split open on the lower side.

237. *Eriodictyon californicum* and related species (7) (Waterleaf Family) Yerba Santa, Mountain Balm

Preparation and Uses: A bitter, but refreshing tea may be made from the dried leaves. When used in strength and quantity it is reported to relieve sore throat, cough, and bronchial congestion. The fresh leaves may be crushed and used as a poultice.

Description: Yerba Santa is a shrubby, aromatic, evergreen plant with shredding bark, and alternate, pinnately veined, irregularly toothed, rather leathery, lanceolate to oblong leaves. The many white to purple flowers occur in flattopped clusters.

Habitat and Distribution: Yerba Santa is found in dry open ground from southern Oregon to southern California.

238. *Amoreuxia palmatifida* and *gonzalezii* (2) (no common name)

*Sarcostemma
cynanchoides*
Climbing Milkweed
236

237

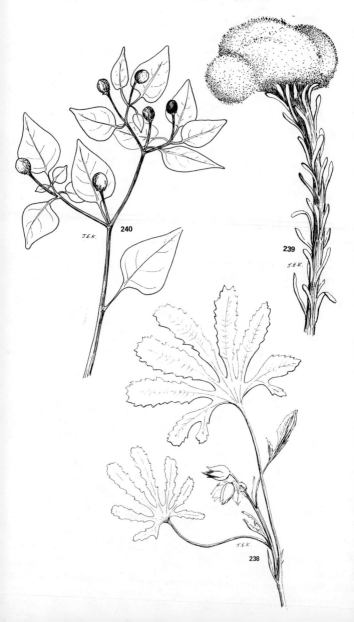

Preparation and Uses: The roots may be roasted or boiled and then eaten, resembling carrots or parsnips in flavor. The fruits also may be eaten.

Habitat and Distribution: These plants are found on rocky slopes and mesas in southern Arizona on south into Mexico.

Description: These herbs have short, flowering stems rising from a large, tuberous root. The leaves have long petioles and are palmately divided into rather wedgeshaped lobes. The large, somewhat irregular, few in number, individually stalked flowers are borne along the upper part of the stem. There are 2 kinds of stamens: one set is long and bears purple anthers; the other set is short and bears yellow anthers. The petals are orange, most of them bearing 1 or 2 large red spots.

239. *Ammobroma sonorae* (1) (Lennoaceae Family)
Sand Food, Sand Root

Preparation and Uses: The long, succulent, underground stems of this root parasite were once used by the Papago Indians as a very nutritious food. The stems are best eaten raw, roasted, or dried and ground into a meal. The meal can be mixed into stew, made into pancakes, eaten as mush, or stored for future use.

Habitat and Distribution: Sand Food is found below 500 feet elevation in drifting sand in southwestern Arizona, southeastern California and northern Sonora.

Description: This plant is a root-parasite having no chlorophyll. The thick, succulent stems are underground. The leaves are reduced to mere scales. The small, numerous flowers are borne on an expanded axis.

240. *Capsicum baccatum* (1) (Borage Family)
Red Pepper, Chillipiquin

Preparation and Uses: The berries or peppers may be used in seasoning or in other ways as a peppery spice. They may be applied medicinally directly to the skin as a skin stimulant.

Habitat and Distribution: Red Pepper is found in southern New Mexico and Arizona on south into Mexico.

Description: This is a more or less shrubby plant with widely branched stems. The slender-petioled, thin, entire, egg-shaped leaves have a tapering point. The slender flower stalks are often in pairs bearing whitish flowers. The globe-shaped berries remain on the plant for some time.

241. *Lycium pallidum* and related species
(14) (Nightshade Family)
Wolf Berry, Desert Thorn, Squaw Berry,
Tomatillo

Preparation and Uses: All western species of this genus produce edible berries, but some are better tasting and juicier than others. The berries are in general insipid and slightly bitter. They may be eaten raw, or cooked up into a sauce. They are best when boiled with a little sugar or put in stews and soups. The berries last well when dried and ground into meal.

Some Old World species are identified by the common name of Matrimony Vine. Their berries are also edible. In the Old World the young leaves of Matrimony Vine are often used as a potherb.

Habitat and Distribution: Wolf Berry is found in the more arid areas of western Texas to southern Colorado and Utah, throughout Arizona and New Mexico, to southern California, and south into Mexico.

Description: These shrubby, spiny, plants may grow either spreading or erect, with entire to minutely toothed leaves that often grow in bundles.

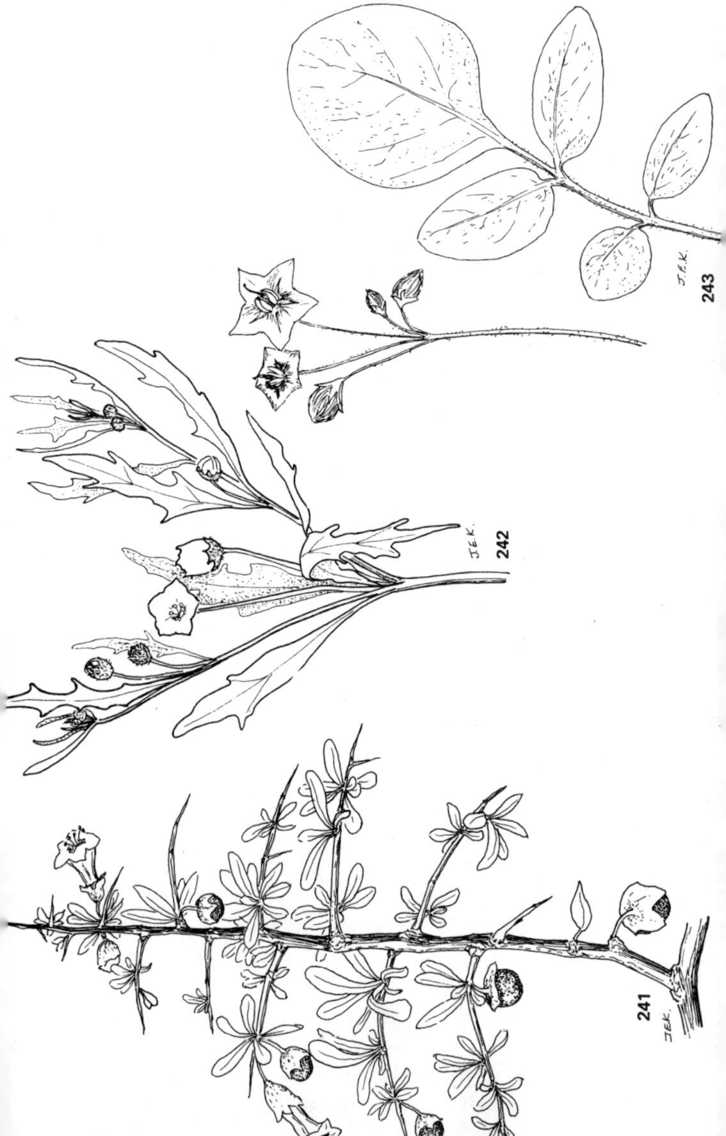
J.E.K.
243
J.E.K.
242
241
J.E.K.

The purple to greenish-purple flowers are borne solitary, or in small clusters in the leaf axils. The roundish berries are fleshy to dry, depending on the species, and, to a lesser degree, on the local growing conditions.

242. *Chamaesaracha coronopus*
(1) (Nightshade Family) (No common name)

Preparation and Uses: The berries may be eaten raw, cooked, or dried, and were so used by the Navajo and Hopi Indians of northern Arizona.

Habitat and Distribution: The plant is found on dry plains and mesas, often among Pinon and Juniper in southern Colorado, Utah, southern Nevada, southern California, and throughout Arizona.

Description: This is a low perennial herb with prostrate branches and leafy stems. The solitary, axillary flowers are on slender stalks, which with fruit are curved backward or downward. The flower is wheel-shaped with hairy cushion-like outgrowths in the throat alternating with the stamens. The berry is closely surrounded, but not covered, by the calyx.

243. *Solanum fendleri* and *jamesii*
(2) (Nightshade Family)
Wild Potato, Indian Potato

Preparation and Uses: These two species have tubers that are similar, though much smaller, to our cultivated potato, *S. tuberosum,* and may be prepared in the same way. It should be remembered that human death has resulted from improper use of the cultivated potato. Potato vines, sprouts, and especially the sprouts and sun-greened skin of the tuber itself are high in solanine, an alkaloid Poisoning has also resulted from eating spoiled potatoes, although this may be due in part to the presence of decay organisms such as fungi or bac teria. All potatoes purchased in the market contain some solanine, but it is in low concentration and tends to be leached out, or perhaps even destroyed, by cooking. Many people like to nibble on raw potatoes, but practically no one eats enough to do any harm, nor does anyone eat the raw peel, which contains most of the solanine of a normal tuber. In general, the sprouts and all greened skin and flesh of the potato should be removed before use.

Solanine poisoning can cause a variety of effects such as drowsiness, trembling, weakness or paralysis, leading to unconsciousness or death. Digestive upset may or may not be severe. When it does occur, nausea, abdominal pain, and other symptoms appear.

Many *Solanum* species have poisonous berries in which solanine is the toxic agent. *S. triflorum* produces berries that are said to be poisonous, particularly when unripe, although they are reported to be eaten by the Zuni Indians. This same species is planted by the Hopi alongside their watermelons in the belief that it will stimulate the growth of the melons. The cultivated wonderberry, a species of *Solanum*, produces berries that are used for preserves and desserts. The wonderberry was once considered to be a cultivated form of *S. nigrum*, a native species, but this is not the case. The berries of *S. nigrum* should be avoided as they are not consistently, if ever, free of solanine. Some confusion as to which species is which adds to the problem of safely eating berries of *Solanum* species.

Habitat and Distribution: *S. fendleri* (Wild Potato) is found in rich soil in open pine forests in New Mexico and Arizona. *S. jamesii* (Indian Potato) is found in mountains in Colorado, Utah, New Mexico, and Arizona.

Description: These herbaceous plants have leafy stems rising from rootstocks bearing tubers. The leaves of the two species listed above are divided into leaflets which in S. *fendleri* are oval to roundish, and in S. *jamesii* are usually narrowly lanceolate. The flowers of S. *fendleri* are usually violet and 5-toothed, while those of S. *jamesii* are usually white and deeply 5-cleft.

244. *Tecoma stans* (1) (Bignonia Family)
Trumpet Bush

Preparation and Uses: The roots may be crushed in water and allowed to ferment for a few days to make a sort of beer. This is still done in Mexico where the roots are also used as a home medicine. The stems and leaves contain some rubber. Trumpet Bush is often seen growing as an ornamental in the warmer areas of the United States.

Habitat and Distribution: Trumpet Bush is found in dry, stony, or gravelly slopes in southern New Mexico and Arizona, and on south into tropical America.

Description: This shrub bears pinnate, opposite leaves divided into 5 or more, lanceolate, toothed leaflets. The funnel-shaped flower is bright yellow.

245. *Proboscidea* species (4) (Martynia Family)
Unicorn Plant, Devil's Claws

Preparation and Uses: The young pods may be boiled and eaten.

Habitat and Distribution: Unicorn Plant is found on plains, mesas, and roadsides from western Texas to southern Nevada, Arizona, southern California, and northern Mexico.

Description: This is a coarse, sticky, hairy annual. The few flowers are showy, and purplish, pinkish, or yellow in color. The large, petioled, mostly opposite leaves are entire to shallowly lobed.

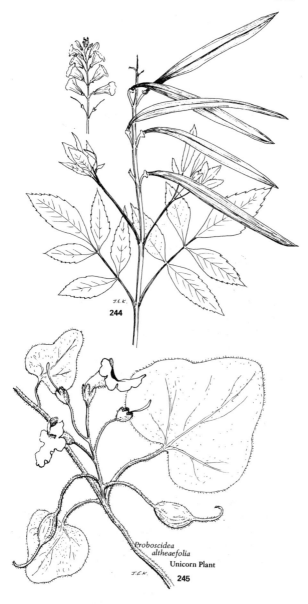

244

*Proboscidea
altheaefolia*
Unicorn Plant

245

246. *Beloperone californica* (1) (Acanthus Family)
Chuparosa

Preparation and Uses: The flowers may be eaten raw or cooked.

Habitat and Distribution: Chuparosa is found on rocky slopes and washes along streams 1000 to 4000 feet in elevation in southeastern California, southern Arizona and northwestern Mexico.

Description: Chuparosa is a shrub with spreading and often leafless branches which are a greenish gray due to the presence of fine whitish hairs. The flowers are a dull red and axillary in position. Stamens number 2, project beyond the flower, and the anther compartments are unequal.

247. *Poliomintha incana* (1) (Mint Family)
Rosemary Mint

Preparation and Uses: The plant may be eaten raw, boiled, or dried, and the flowers used for seasoning.

Habitat and Distribution: *P. incana* is found in sandy ground in southern California, Arizona, Utah, New Mexico, and probably southwestern Colorado.

Description: This shrub is densely covered with felt-like hairs. The stems bear linear to oblong, entire leaves. The blue, rose or purple flowers are in small, axillary clusters near the ends of the branches.

248. *Hyptis emoryi* (1) (Mint Family)
Desert Lavender

Preparation and Uses: The seeds may be eaten parched, or ground into flour.

Habitat and Distribution: This plant is found on dry, rocky slopes and canyons in southern Arizona, California, and northwestern Mexico.

Description: Desert Lavender is an erect, aromatic shrub with opposite, toothed, oval-shaped leaves that have somewhat wavy margins. The slender, rather straight branches are whitish in color and covered with small, knobby or bran-like scales, and densely matted with soft hairs.

249. *Cowania mexicana* (1) (Rose Family)
Cliffrose, Quinine Bush

Preparation and Uses: A refreshing tea may be made by steeping a handful of the leaves in hot water for a few minutes. A strong tea can be used as an emetic and for washing wounds.

Indians of Nevada and Utah shredded and braided the bark into clothing, sandals, mats, and rope. The Hopi used the wood for making arrows.

Habitat and Distribution: Cliffrose is common on dry slopes and mesas, particularly in Pinon-Juniper woodland, from southern Colorado across Utah and Nevada to California, south through New Mexico, Arizona, and southeastern California to central Mexico.

Description: Cliffrose is a much branched shrub with reddish-brown or greenish twigs above, older twigs with shredding gray bark below. The alternate, simple, leathery leaves are gland-dotted and resinous. The large, white, creamy to yellow, 5-petaled flowers are at the ends of short branches.

250. *Prunus ilicifolia* (1) (Rose Family)
Islay, Holly-leaved Cherry

Preparation and Uses: The fruit is pleasant tasting, and the large pit may be used after proper preparation to remove the cyanide. The pit should be dried in the sun, then cracked, the kernel removed and crushed or ground, and leached in running water for several hours. After this it may be

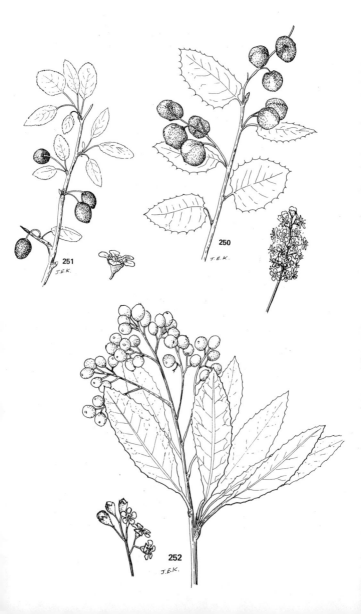

251

250

252

eaten as mush, or dried and stored.

Habitat and Distribution: Islay is common on dry slopes and alluvial fans in southern California on to Baja California.

Description: Islay is a dense, evergreen shrub or small tree growing from 3 to 25 feet tall. The smooth twigs are gray to reddish brown in color. The tough, leathery, roundish leaves bear stiff spiny teeth around the edges. The few to many white flowers are borne in racemes. The fruit is usually red, but occasionally yellow.

251. *Prunus subcordata* (1) (Rose Family)
Sierra Plum, Western Plum

Preparation and Uses: The slightly acid pulp of the fruit is pleasant to the taste. The amount of pulp varies with locality according to the water supply. In some areas the fruit will be quite fleshy and in others too dry to be good eating.

Habitat and Distribution: Sierra Plum is found on dry to moist, rocky slopes from southern Oregon west of the Cascades to southern California.

Description: The plant is a stout, crooked-branched shrub or small tree, often spiny. The roundish to oval leaves are unevenly finely toothed. The white to pink flowers develop into a dark-red to yellow fruit.

252. *Heteromeles arbutifolia* (1) (Rose Family)
Toyon Berry, Christmas Berry

Preparation and Uses: The berries are edible raw, toasted, steamed, or boiled and are best with a little sugar added. Cider may also be made from the berries in much the same way as the manzanita.

Habitat and Distribution: Toyon Berries are found in dry ground at lower elevations from northern to southern California.

Description: The plant is an evergreen shrub occasionally reaching thirty feet in height. The toothed, simple leaves are dark green, tough, and leathery. The flowers are small, white and numerous. Sepals and petals number 5. The petals are spreading, rounded, and concave. Stamens number 10 and occur in pairs opposite the sepals. The fruit is berrylike and pulpy; it is usually red but is sometimes yellow.

253. *Peteria scoparia* (1) (**Pea Family**)
Camote-de-Monte

Preparation and Uses: The tuberous rootstocks may be eaten roasted or boiled.

Habitat and Distribution: Camote-de-Monte is found from western Texas to northeastern Arizona.

Description: The plant is an herbaceous perennial with low, stiff, slender stems bearing pinnately divided leaves. The numerous, small leaflets have spiny stipules. The flowers are in tall, open racemes.

254. *Mimosa biuncifera* (1) (**Pea Family**)
Catclaw Mimosa

Preparation and Uses: The edible pods are best when dried, ground into meal, and used as mush or cakes.

Habitat and Distribution: This shrub is found in dry soil on mesas and rocky slopes from western Texas to Arizona and northern Mexico.

Description: Catclaw Mimosa is a stout, spined shrub. The leaves are distinctive with their numerous, small leaflets. The small, pale pink to white flowers are borne in many-flowered heads. The pods are somewhat curved.

255. *Acacia greggii* (1) (**Pea Family**)
Catclaw Acacia, Devil's Claw

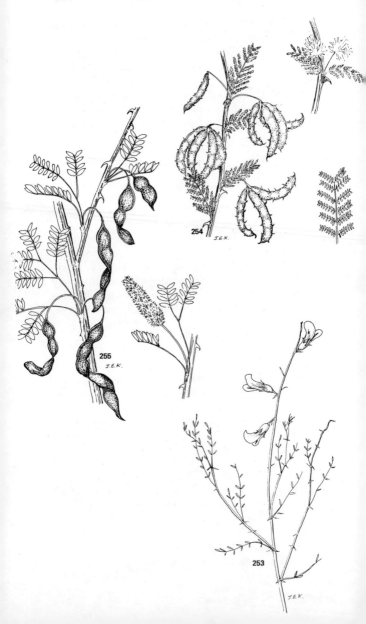

Preparation and Uses: A nutritious meal may be ground from the dried pods. The meal may then be used in mush or cakes, or in other ways.

Habitat and Distribution: Catclaw Acacia is found in desert areas in southern and western Arizona, and southern and southeastern California up to 4500 feet, often forming thickets along streams and washes. It is also found in the Grand Canyon and Havasu Canyon of northern Arizona.

Description: This is a straggly, much branched shrub or small tree sometimes reaching 20 feet in height. The branches have short, stiff, curved spines. The tiny, yellow flowers are in dense clusters 1 to 2 inches long and appear from April to October. The leaves are twice pinnately divided into small, oblong leaflets. The pods are brown, 2 to 6 inches long, flattened, mostly curved, and often twisted. They ripen in the fall and often remain on the branches for long periods.

256a. *Prosopis juliflora* (1) (**Pea Family**)
Mesquite, Honey Mesquite

Preparation and Uses: The long, sweet pods may be ground into a meal which may be prepared as cakes, mush, etc. The meal can be mixed with water to provide a refreshing non-alcoholic beverage, or allowed to ferment to make an intoxicating drink. A sweet beverage can also be made by first boiling the whole pods in water, then mashing them in fresh water and straining out the residue. The remaining liquid is then ready to drink. Another preparation is to soak the seeds for several hours in water to produce a sweet lemon flavored drink.

The pod, minus the hard seeds, can be eaten raw or cooked, and is sweet. The gum that is exuded from the bark can be eaten as is, or made into candy. A black dye can be obtained from it. The Indians pounded and shredded the inner bark

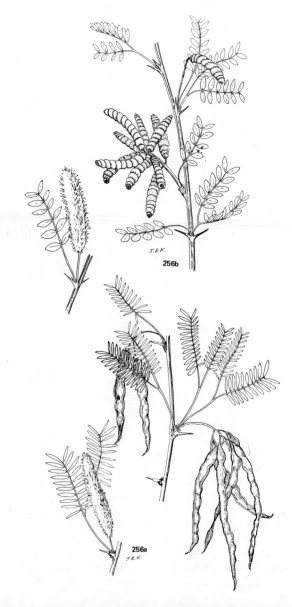

256b

256a

to use in basketry and coarse fabrics.

Habitat and Distribution: Mesquite is found chiefly along streams and in areas from southern Kansas west to southeastern California and northwestern Mexico where the water table is relatively high.

Description: The plant is a shrub or small tree and grows to 25 feet; it usually has spines. The leaves bear numerous narrow leaflets. The small greenish-yellow flowers are rather fragrant and are borne in cylindrical spikes. The fruits are flat and pod-like, not coiled, and are more or less restricted between the seeds; they grow to 6 inches in length.

256b. *Prosopis pubescens* (1) (Pea Family)
Screwbean, Tornillo

Preparation and Uses: The cooked pods are even sweeter than those of Mesquite. They can be boiled down to an excellent, sweet syrup. Screwbean meal can be used in the same ways as can Mesquite, except that here the seeds are also used.

Habitat and Distribution: Screwbean is found along washes and streams, and on flood plains, often in saline soil, from western Texas to southern Nevada, southern California, and northern Mexico.

Description: As one might expect, this plant is extremely similar to Mesquite. The leaflets, however, are not as narrow in comparison to their length as Mesquite. Probably the most distinctive feature is the tightly coiled, spring-like pod from which comes the name of Screwbean.

257. *Cercis occidentalis* (1) (Pea Family)
Redbud, Judas Tree

Preparation and Uses: The flowers have a sharp, acid flavor and are good in salads. The flower buds may be pickled. The buds, flowers, and young

257

258

259

pods are good fried in butter or made into fritters.

The astringent bark may be used raw to treat diarrhea. Some California Indian groups used the strong, pliable bark in weaving baskets.

Habitat and Distribution: Redbud is found on dry slopes and in canyons and foothills in California, Nevada, Utah and Arizona.

Description: The plant is a large shrub to small tree reaching from 6 to 30 feet in height. The clustered stems and branches are borne erect. The leaves are rounded to kidney-shaped, hairless, entire, and heart-shaped at the base. The extremely showy red-purple flowers appear before the leaves in the spring.

258. *Cercidium microphyllum* and *floridum*
(2) (Pea Family)
Palo Verde

Preparation and Uses: The seeds of this small tree may be ground into a nutritious meal.

Habitat and Distribution: Palo Verde is common along washes and on flood plains, and less frequent on dry lower slopes in southern and western Arizona, southeastern California, Sonora, and Baja California.

Description: These plants are large shrubs or small trees, reaching about 25 feet in height. The young bark is smooth and green. The tree is leafless in the dry season but retains its green bark. The bipinnate leaves have cylindrical stalks. The yellow flowers are in short, axillary clusters. The clawed petals number 5; there are 10 distinct stamens. The several-seeded, linear to oblong seed pod is often reddish in color.

259. *Hoffmannseggia densiflora* (1) (Pea Family)
Camote-de-Raton, Hog Potato, Rushpea

Preparation and Uses: The tuberous enlargements of the roots may be eaten after roasting or boiling.

Habitat and Distribution: Hog Potato is found in open ground from Kansas to Arizona, Colorado, and southern California.

Description: The plant is an herbaceous perennial, 5 to 16 inches tall, with bipinnate, gland-dotted leaves. The leaflets are small. The scattered stems rise from underground rootstocks. The 5-petaled flower is yellow with 10 stamens, and occurs in racemes.

260. *Psoralea esculenta, megalantha, mephitica* and *ep…psila* (4) (Pea Family)
Bread Root, Scurf Pea, Indian Turnip

Preparation and Uses: These four species have tuberous roots that are edible when cooked.

Habitat and Distribution: The plants are found on hills and mesas in southwestern Colorado, southern Utah, and northern Arizona.

Description: Bread Roots are perennial herbs with thick roots from which rise flowering stems. The 3 to 5 leaflets are clustered at the end of the petiole.

261. *Dalea terminalis* (1) (Pea Family)
Pea Bush, Smokethorn.(No illustration shown)

Preparation and Uses: The roots of this plant are very sweet when eaten raw, and were used by the Hopi. The seeds may be eaten parched or ground into flour.

A yellow-brown dye may be obtained from *D. emoryi* by steeping the glandular twigs in hot water. The seeds of this species may also be eaten.

Habitat and Distribution: Pea Bush is found in sandy soil from western Texas to southern Utah, Arizona and Chihuahua.

Description: Pea Bush is a prostrate herb with 7 to 15 odd-pinnate leaves. The purple flowers have clawed petals and are borne in terminal spikes that are usually elongate and relatively slender, being 1¼ to 3¼ inches long and rarely more than ¼ inch wide. The plant is entirely herbaceous, being completely without any woody tissue such as occurs in some other species of *Dalea*. Pea Bush is exceedingly hairy throughout except for the hairless calyx tube. The leaflets are obovate. The bracts are broadly obovate, have an abruptly tapering point, and are very obviously glandular-punctate.

262. *Olneya tesota* (1) (Pea Family)
Tesota, Ironwood, Desert Ironwood

Preparation and Uses: The parched or roasted seeds are nutritious and have a peanut-like flavor. They are still collected by people living in our southwestern deserts.

The wood is extremely hard and is sometimes used for tool handles. It was formerly used by southwestern Indians for making arrowheads.

Habitat and Distribution: Tesota is common in washes and along streams in southern Arizona, southeastern California, Sonora, and Baja California.

Description: Tesota is a spiny tree with thin, scaly bark and dense, evergreen foliage, producing an overall grayish hue. The pinnate leaves are divided into 8 to 24 leaflets, densely covered with white hairs. Below each leaf is a pair of spines. The few flowers occur in axillary racemes and appear each year before the new growth of leaves. The pods are thick and bulging.

263. *Robinia neomexicana* and *pseudo-acacia*
(2) (Pea Family)
New Mexican Locust, Locust, Black Locust

Preparation and Uses: About the only thing one may be sure of with these plants is that the flowers may be gathered and fried. Various writers have reported that the inner bark, roots, and seeds may be eaten, but this writer believes these reports to be in error. Too many reliably reported cases of poisoning have occurred from eating the bark, roots, and seeds to tempt one's health by using them.

The Hopi Indians use the plant to treat rheumatism and as an emetic.

Habitat and Distribution: The Locust is found in canyons and coniferous forests in southern Colorado to southern Nevada, western Texas, New Mexico, Arizona, and northern Mexico.

Description: Locusts are large, thorny shrubs to small trees bearing pinnately divided leaves with numerous leaflets. The large, showy, purple-pink flowers are borne in dense racemes.

264. *Phaseolus acutifolius, metcalfei* and related species
(10) (Pea Family)
Tepary Bean, Bean

Preparation and Uses: The beans of the two species listed above are particularly good when cooked, but other species are of value too. The Tepary Bean is a form of *P. acutifolius,* which is grown extensively by the Papago Indians and others in the Southwest. Even though domesticated this native plant is common in the wild.

Several other species, native to the New World but not to the United States, are widely cultivated. The String Bean, *P. vulgaris,* and the Lima Bean, *P. lunatus,* are two notable examples.

As seems so often to be the case with some of our most widely cultivated plants, beans can be poisonous. All species contain cyanide in the seed. Fortunately, virtually all of the cyanide is driven off by cooking, rendering the seed or green pods edible.

263
J.E.K.

264
J.E.K.

The cyanide content varies from species to species and is difficult to remove from some, such as the small, black Puerto Rican lima bean, which has caused some human deaths on that island. Our native species are quite safe after proper cooking.

Habitat and Distribution: These plants are found in many habitats due to their spread by man for cultivation. In the wild they are common among the live-oaks, and at the lower limit of the pine belt in southern New Mexico, Arizona and on south into Mexico.

Description: Bean plants are herbaceous perennials or annuals, usually with long, trailing stems. The leaves are pinnately trifoliate. The axillary flowers are usually in racemes and vary in color from white to pink to deep purple or even brick red.

265.   *Juglans major, californica,* and *hindsii*
       (3) (Walnut Family)
       Walnut

   Preparation and Uses: The small, thick-shelled nuts are good eaten raw.
   Habitat and Distribution: These native walnuts are commonly found along streams and washes in New Mexico, Arizona, the warmer areas of California, and northern Mexico.
   Description: Our native walnuts are trees or large shrubs with aromatic, pinnately compound leaves, commonly with 9 to 13 large leaflets. The hard-shelled fruit is that of a typical walnut, being encased in a more or less pulpy husk. The edible nuts are within the thick shell.

266.   *Populus fremontii* (1) (Willow Family)
       Cottonwood, Fremont Cottonwood

   Preparation and Uses: The catkins may be eaten

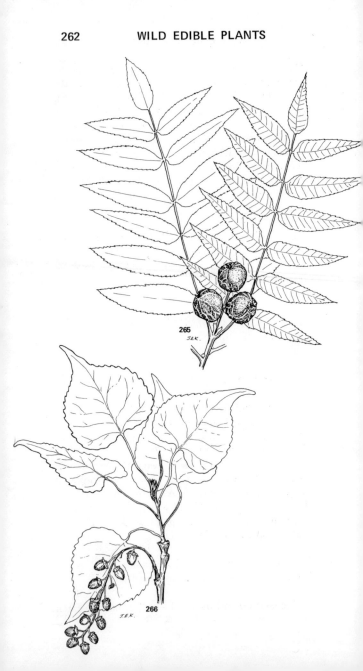

265

J.E.K.

266

J.E.K.

raw, or boiled in stews. The inner bark of any of the many trees in this genus can be eaten and it was often used as an emergency food by western Indians.

Habitat and Distribution: Fremont Cottonwood is found along streams and in washes from western Texas through New Mexico, Arizona and Nevada, into California and northern Mexico.

Description: The tree is a typical cottonwood from 36 to 90 or 100 feet tall, with grayish-white, rough bark, and stout, hairless twigs. The coarsely serrate, hairless leaves are triangular in shape. The catkins are 1½ to 2 inches long.

267. *Morus microphylla* (1) (Mulberry Family)
Mulberry, Texas Mulberry

Preparation and Uses: The tart fruits may be eaten raw, and are excellent in pies and jellies. The Papago Indians of southern Arizona still use them.

Habitat and Distribution: The Mulberry is usually found along streams and in washes where there is sufficient underground moisture, from western Texas to Arizona and northern Mexico.

Description: The Mulberry is a large shrub or small tree seldom exceeding 15 feet in height. Its alternate leaves are palmately lobed, especially on new shoots. However, the leaf shape for the entire tree is quite variable. The sexes of the flowers are separate but both are in catkins. The pistillate flowers become a thick, succulent, juicy, elongated berry.

268. *Vitis californica, arizonica,* and related species
(4) (Grape Family)
Western Wild Grape, Canyon Grape

Preparation and Uses: The grapes are edible raw and may be used in the same manner as domestic

269
J.E.K.

267
J.E.K.

268
J.E.K.

grapes.   Since the time of the classical Greeks,
grape leaves and various concoctions of the berries
have been valued medicinally.   In various parts of
the world, including the West in pioneer times,
grape leaves soaked in water were used as a poultice for wounds.   The leaves were said to be good
when used in this way externally, and when taken
internally, were cures for snake bite and disorders
of the internal organs.   Juice squeezed from the
leaves was presumed to cure loose bowels in everyone, and lust in women.

Habitat and Distribution: The several grape
species are found in the greater Southwest, including southwestern Oregon, southern Colorado, Utah,
and Nevada, through California into Mexico.

Description: Wild grapes are exactly like their
cultivated cousins, although usually smaller leaved,
and bearing smaller, though juicy, fruits.   They are
woody vines with climbing tendrils opposite the
palmately lobed or toothed, broad, green leaves.
The berries have the typical grape appearance, and
are purple when ripe.

269.   *Rhamnus crocea* (1) (Buckthorn Family)
Buckthorn

Preparation and Uses: The nutritious berries
may be eaten raw and are excellent cooked with
meat.   However, it is reported that they will turn
the skin red temporarily, if eaten in quantity.

Two closely related species *R. californica* (Coffee-
berry) and *R. purshiana* (Cascara Sagrada), are effective laxatives.   *R. purshiana* is used in commercial medicinal preparations.   The bark provides one
of the most gentle and best laxatives known.   It
should be collected in the fall or spring and dried
for a year or more.   For a laxative, hot water is
poured on a level teaspoonful of powdered bark
and drunk when cool.   Fresh bark will work well

when boiled for several hours. For a tonic and to improve the appetite, some old-timers recommend soaking some of the dried bark overnight in a glass of water and then drinking the water on rising.

Habitat and Distribution: Buckthorn is common in chaparral and in open coniferous forest in California, Arizona and Baja California.

Description: The plant is a spreading, evergreen, much branched shrub with bright-green, hollylike leaves and red fruit. Usually it reaches from 3 to 7 feet in height, but occasionally it is found nearly 30 feet tall.

270. *Simmondsia chinensis* (1) (Box Family)
Jojoba, Deer Nut, Goat Nut

Preparation and Uses: The bitter nuts contain a nutritious oil and may be eaten raw, roasted, or parched. The bitter flavor is due to tannin. The nuts were once used as a substitute for coffee, prepared as follows: roast the seeds and grind the kernels together with the yolk of a hard-boiled egg; boil this pasty mass in water for several minutes; add sugar and cream or milk; flavor with vanilla for a savory drink. Of course, if you are a purist, you can drink it black!

The oil of these nuts was formerly used in the manufacture of hair oil, and as a substitute for beeswax in electrical insulation, varnishes, and phonograph records.

Habitat and Distribution: Jojoba is common on dry slopes and along washes in southern Arizona, southern California, and on south into Sonora and Baja California.

Description: This plant is a highly branched, evergreen shrub, with entire, simple, thick, leathery, opposite leaves. The small, greenish-yellow flowers are borne in dense, short, axillary clusters. The brown fruit is acorn-like.

270

271

271. *Aesculus californica* (1) (Buckeye Family)
Buckeye, California Buckeye

Preparation and Uses: When raw and untreated the nuts of this plant are quite poisonous and were used by various California Indians to stupify fish so that they could be more easily caught.

The nuts were also used as food. One wonders how many people died before the trial and error process of rendering the nuts edible became wholly and consistently successful.

There are a number of ways of processing the fleshy nuts. One is as follows: the shiny brown nuts are first steamed in a fire-pit for several hours until they are the texture of boiled potatoes; they are then sliced thinly, placed in a basket and soaked in running water for 2 to 5 days, depending on the thickness of the slices, to remove the poison.

Another way is to steam them, remove the skin, mash them, and mix them with water to form a thin paste. This is then soaked from 1 to 10 hours in a sand filter or running water.

The residue from either process is high in starch, quite nutritious, and not bad in flavor. It may be eaten cold or baked into bread or cakes.

Habitat and Distribution: The Buckeye is found only in California in the foothills of the Coast Ranges and Sierras on dry hillsides and in canyons.

Description: The plant is a large shrub or small tree growing up to 25 feet high. The opposite, palmate leaves have 5 to 7 oblong to lanceolate leaflets with lightly saw-edge margins. The white flowers are in candle-like spikes. The fruits are large, brownish or greenish balls inside of which is a shiny dark brown nut containing white meat.

272. *Acer grandidentatum* (1) (Maple Family)
Big-tooth Maple

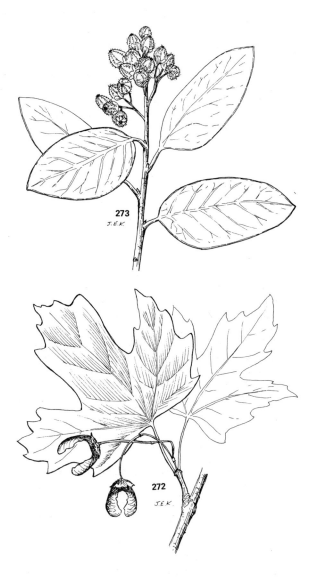

273
J.E.K.

272
J.E.K.

Preparation and Uses: Maple syrup can be made by boiling down the sap of this western species.

Habitat and Distribution: This maple is found in valleys, canyons, and slopes from 4500 to 7000 feet in Montana, Wyoming, Idaho to western Texas, New Mexico and Arizona.

Description: Big-tooth Maple is often more shrubby than tree-like and grows to 15 feet in height. The thin bark is dark brown or gray. The typical maple leaves are 2 to 5 inches across, fairly round in outline, dark green above, pale and hairy underneath, deeply 3-lobed, and very coarsely toothed. The winged seeds are paired.

273. *Rhus ovata* (1) (Sumac Family)
Sugar Bush

Preparation and Uses: The berries may be soaked in water to make a sweetish, flavorful drink.

Habitat and Distribution: Sugar Bush is found on slopes and mesas, commonly in the chaparral, from central Arizona to southern California and Baja California.

Description: Sugar Bush is an evergreen shrub with stout, reddish branches bearing tough, leathery, oval leaves, often somewhat folded along the midrib. The flowers are borne in dense clusters: the fruit is reddish.

274a. *Cymopterus newberryi* (1) (Carrot Family)
Corkwing, Wafer Parsnip

Preparation and Uses: In spring the roots may be eaten raw as sweets. Later they lose their sweetness but remain edible.

Habitat and Distribution: Corkwing is usually found in sandy soil in southern Utah, northern Arizona, and southwestern Colorado.

Description: This is a perennial plant rising from an elongated, thickened taproot that often bears underground stems. The leaves are thin and fleshy, and variable in form, being often highly lobed, or with lobed leaflets about as wide as long. The yellow flowers are clustered at the ends of stems that are longer than the petioles.

274b. *Cymopterus purpurascens* (1) (Carrot Family)
Gamote, Camote

Preparation and Uses: The parsnip-like root is edible cooked and was much used by southwestern Indians. It is still used extensively in Mexico, where it is claimed that the root is sweeter and more tender than the garden parsnip.

Habitat and Distribution: Gamote is found in dry, often rocky ground in southern Idaho, south through Nevada to southeastern California, through Arizona into Mexico, and east through Utah to western Colorado.

Description: Gamote is an essentially stemless perennial rising from a slender taproot. The bi-pinnate to pinnate, oval to oblong, hairless, pale leaves have rounded to sharp pointed lobes.

275. *Cucurbita foetidissima* (1) (Gourd Family)
Buffalo Gourd, Calabazilla

Preparation and Uses: The gourd may be eaten cooked, or dried for future use. When ground, the seeds may be eaten as mush. Both the raw gourd and the root of this plant yield a good cleansing lather when crushed in water and rubbed between the hands.

Habitat and Distribution: Buffalo Gourd is found in varied habitats, mostly in dry ground in southern Colorado, New Mexico, Arizona, southern California and south into Mexico.

Description: Buffalo Gourd is an odorous, rough, coarse perennial with huge spindle-shaped roots,

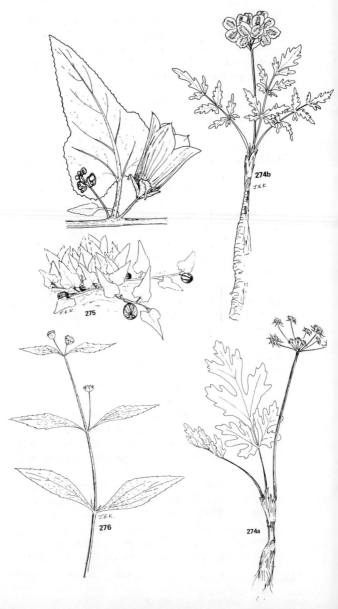

from which rise trailing stems bearing large, triangular leaves that are often sharply heart-shaped. The large, yellow, axillary flowers are solitary. The fruit is a typical gourd, often rather egg-shaped and cream-white with green stripes.

276. *Eclipta alba* (1) (Sunflower Family)
Eclipta

   Preparation and Uses: The entire plant above ground may be used as a potherb.
   Habitat and Distribution: Eclipta is found growing along streams, ditches, lake shores, and wet banks throughout the Southwest.
   Description: Although the plant is an annual herb, it may be found growing all months of the year. It is low growing, bearing lanceolate, toothed or entire, opposite leaves. The white flowers are in heads borne on stalks in the upper axils, and are not conspicuous.

277. *Bidens bipinnata* (1) (Sunflower Family)
Spanish Needles, Beggarticks

   Preparation and Uses: The leaves may be used as a potherb.
   Habitat and Distribution: The plant is found in rich, damp soil in Arizona, New Mexico, Colorado, and probably Nevada and Utah.
   Description: Spanish Needles, reaching from 1 to 3 feet tall, is erect and usually branching, and is hairless or nearly so. The petioled leaves are usually 2 to 3-pinnately divided, the last division being oblong to narrowly triangular. The yellow flowers are in heads. The rays are absent or very small, and are yellowish-white.

278. *Cosmos sulphureus* (1) (Sunflower Family)
Cosmos

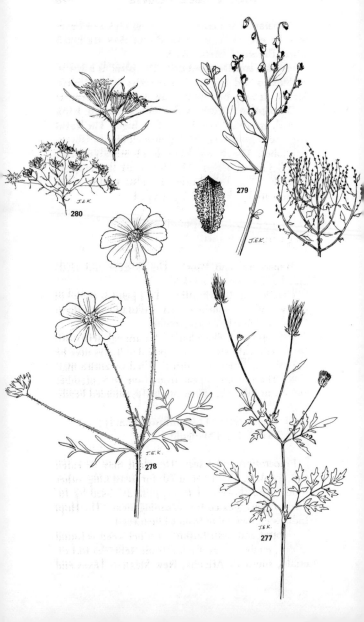

Preparation and Uses: The young tops and leaves may be eaten raw, or in salad, but they are much better flavored when cooked.

Habitat and Distribution: The plant is a native of Mexico and is grown in gardens in the United States. It may be found as an occasional escapee.

Description: Cosmos is a tall, branched, hairy annual, growing from 3 to 6 feet high. The leaves are 2 to 3 pinnately divided into elliptic to lanceolate lobes. The showy flower heads are large, being 1½ to 3 inches across. The showy ray flowers have 3 teeth. The disk flowers are also yellow. The anthers are black and orange tipped.

279. *Dicoria brandegei* (1) (Sunflower Family)
Single-fruited Dicoria

Preparation and Uses: The flowers and seeds may be eaten raw or cooked.

Habitat and Distribution: This plant is found in sandy soil in southwestern Colorado, southern Utah, and northeastern Arizona.

Description: The plant is an annual herb with branched, leafy stems. The petioled leaves may be opposite or alternate, with toothed or entire margins. The flowers appear from June to September and occur in small, numerous, leafy, panicled heads.

280. *Pectis angustifolia* (1) (Sunflower Family)
Chinchweed, Fetid Marigold

Preparation and Uses: The plant may be eaten raw, cooked, dried, or used for seasoning other food. The flowers of *P. papposa* are used by Indians of New Mexico for seasoning meat. The Hopi Indians extract a dye from Chinchweed.

Habitat and Distribution: Chinchweed is found in dry, sandy or gravelly soil from Nebraska to Colorado, south to Arizona, New Mexico, Texas and

Mexico.

Description: The plant is a low, slender-stemmed annual with opposite, entire leaves that are dotted with transparent glands. The flower heads are small and yellow in color. Often the rays are purplish underneath.

281. *Chlorogalum pomeridianum* (1) (Lily Family)
Soap Plant, Amole

Preparation and Uses: The bottle-shaped bulb is deep set in the ground and covered with coarse brown fibers. The bulb may be roasted with the fibers in place, then peeled and eaten, or peeled and boiled and then eaten. The small, young green shoots may be slowly baked or steamed to provide a good nourishing green. The young, fresh green leaves may be eaten raw.

For a cleansing soap, strip off the fibers and crush the heart of the bulb in water; rub vigorously to produce a good lather. This preparation also makes a good shampoo and leaves the hair soft and glossy, and is said to be good for removing dandruff.

The crushed green plant, including the root, can be used in streams to stupify fish, but must be used in quantity.

Habitat and Distribution: Amole is found on dry hills and plains, sometimes in open woods from Southern Oregon to southern California.

Description: The branched stem rises from a large, deep-seated, fiber-coated bulb. Basal leaves number several to many and are tufted, long and linear. Stem leaves are little developed. The flowers are in a panicle with their parts colored white with a green or purple midvein. The plant is 2-4 feet tall.

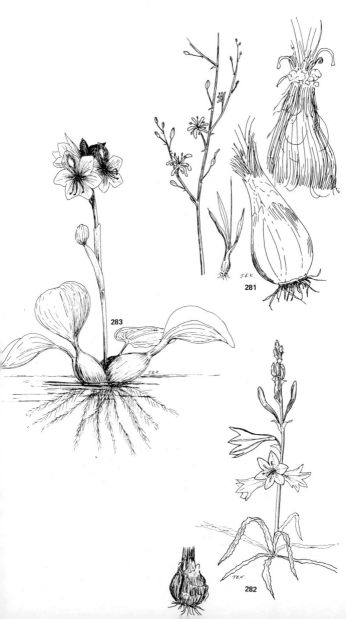

281

283

282

282. *Hesperocallis undulata* (1) (Lily Family)
Desert Lily, Ajo

Preparation and Uses: The bulbs of this plant
may be eaten roasted or boiled, but are not easy to
obtain since they often lie at a depth of 18 inches
or more.

Habitat and Distribution: Desert Lily is found
in sandy soil in southwestern Arizona and adjacent
California deserts.

Description: This stout, straight-stemmed plant
is leafy at the base and rises from an oval-shaped
bulb. The linear leaves are distinctive in being blue-
green in color. The white flowers are borne in a terminal raceme.

283. *Eichhornia crassipes* (1) (Pickerel-Weed Family)
Water Hyacinth

Preparation and Uses: The young leaves, leaf
stalks, flower stalks, and flower buds may be eaten
after thorough steaming or boiling. If not boiled
long enough, the plant may cause unpleasant itching of the skin after being eaten.

Water Hyacinth is a beautiful-flowered native of
tropical America and has been introduced to many
of the warmer areas of the world, often to become
a serious impediment to water-way navigation. It
was introduced to the southeastern United States
from Brazil.

Habitat and Distribution: In the West, Water
Hyacinth has become occasionally naturalized in
sloughs and slow water in the San Joaquin River
Valley, and in the Santa Ana River system of California.

Description: Water Hyacinth is a floating, herbaceous perennial. The bright green leaves grow up
directly from the roots and are oval to round in
shape. The leaf stalks are quite swollen, being inflated with air-filled spongy tissue near the base,

allowing the plant to float high out of water. The violet to blue flowers appear on a central stem.

284. *Monochoria vaginalis* (1) (Pickerel Weed Family)
Pickerel Weed

Preparation and Uses: The entire plant, including the fruits, above ground may be eaten raw or cooked. The fruits may also be dried and stored. This plant has been introduced from southeast Asia where it is sold on the market.

Habitat and Distribution: According to Munz the plant is found as a weed in Butte County, California, rice-fields.

Description: Pickerel Weed is a perennial herb rising from a short, spongy rootstock. The plant has both basal and stem leaves, the latter being solitary at the top of the stems or branches. The long-petioled leaves are 7 to 9 veined, linear to oval, and are sometimes heart-shaped at the base. The flower is 6-parted, blue in color, and sprinkled with red. There are 6 stamens.

285. *Yucca species* (16) (Agave Family)
Yucca, Spanish Bayonet, Soap Weed, Datil

Preparation and Uses: All of the species are edible, but some are better than others. The flowers, buds, and young flower stalks may be eaten raw, or peeled and boiled, or roasted.

Y. baccata, often called the Banana Yucca, produces large, pulpy fruits which can be eaten raw, roasted, dried, or ground into meal. To some people the Banana Yucca's fruits, when roasted, resemble bananas in flavor. The seeds may also be eaten. The sliced pulp of the fruit makes a good substitute for apples in pie. The pulp, minus the fiber, can be boiled down to a paste, rolled out in inch thick sheets and dried. This can be eaten as is or dissolved

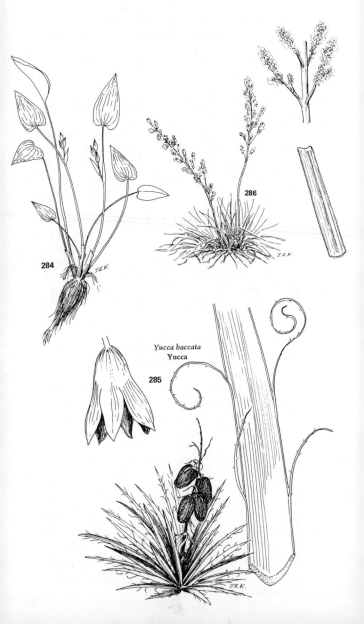

Yucca baccata
Yucca

284

286

285

in water to make a refreshing beverage. A sufficient quantity of it dissolved in water results in an excellent syrup.

The flower stalk of most species is best eaten when full grown but just before the buds expand. The stalk should be cut into sections, and eaten boiled or roasted. The tough rind is easily removed after cooking.

The roots produce a good lather when cut into convenient lengths, mashed, and rubbed vigorously in water. Such lather imparts a sheen to the hair. The roots may also be used as a laxative. Southwestern Indians obtained fiber from the leaves in the same manner as from the Agave.

Habitat and Distribution: The various species are found in desert areas and in Pinon-Juniper woods in southern Colorado, the southern half or more of Utah and Nevada, all of New Mexico and Arizona, and in southern California.

Description: These plants vary from small shrubs to fairly large trees such as *Y. brevifolia,* the well known Joshua Tree. They have numerous, spine-tipped, narrow, elongate, usually stiff leaves clustered at the end of the trunk or branches, if any. Often the leaves rise from a very short, woody trunk or caudex that is mostly underground. The large, whitish to cream-colored, numerous flowers are in terminal racemes or panicles.

286. *Nolina microcarpa* (1) (Agave Family)
Sacahuista, Bear Grass

Preparation and Uses: Southwestern Indians used the caudex and very young shoots of this plant in the same way as the Agave, but did not eat the flowers or fruit.

All *Nolina* species are reliably reported to be poisonous to livestock, at least when approaching maturity. Poisoning seems to be associated only with the blooms which are greedily eaten by sheep and cattle. The leaves seem to cause no trouble. The poisonous principle is unknown but causes severe liver and kidney damage.

Habitat and Distribution: Sacahuista is found in rolling range land and foothills from western Texas to Arizona and northern Mexico.

Description: This plant has a large, woody caudex with many narrow leaves coming from the base. The stem is leafless. The numerous, brownish-cream flowers are borne in a large, terminal panicle.

287. *Dasylirion wheeleri* (1) (Agave Family)
Sotol, Bear Grass

Preparation and Uses: The budding flower stalks may be roasted and eaten, being prepared in much the same way as the agave. Southwestern Indians, in fact, would often roast these two plants together in an open fire pit. The heads of the plant contain much sugar and have been used in alcohol manufacture. The highly sugary sap of the bud stalk is gathered today in northern Mexico and fermented to make a potent beverage called sotol.

Habitat and Distribution: Sotol is found on the deserts from western Texas to Arizona and northern Mexico.

Description: The plant is yucca-like with a thick, woody, mostly underground caudex. The leaves are in large clusters, very rigid, the margins bearing sharp, curved spines and grow to 3 feet long. The sexes are separate, the flowers being in either pistillate or staminate large terminal panicles. A flower stalk rises from the center of the plant to a height of 5 to 15 feet. The flowers are cream colored.

288. *Agave* species (10) (Agave Family)
Agave, Century Plant

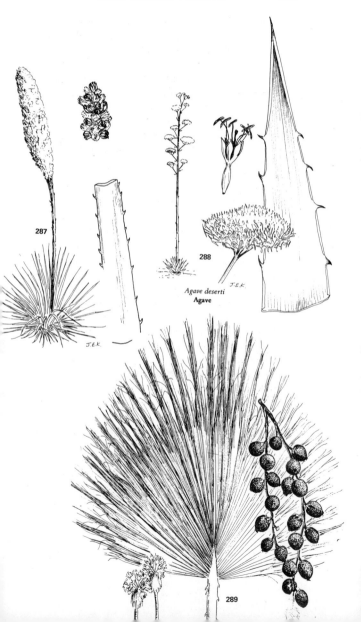

287

288

Agave deserti
Agave

J.E.K.

289

Preparation and Uses: All of the species are edible, but some are better than others. The caudex is eaten roasted or boiled and is best when young. With age it becomes fibrous. The flavor is that of a cross between banana and pineapple, and is quite pleasant. The roasted caudex becomes soft and may be sliced, or mashed, worked into small cakes, and dried for future use. A piece of these cakes boiled in water makes a flavorful beverage. The flowers themselves may be boiled and eaten, or dried. The seeds can be made into flour and used accordingly. The very young leaves may be eaten raw or cooked, but are somewhat fibrous.

In Mexico and Central America, species of *Agave* are grown for their fibers known as henequen or sisal. Other species yield the ingredients for pulque, an intoxicating beverage which is fermented agave juice. Tequila is made by distillation of a fermented mash made from the caudex.

Fibers may be obtained from the leaves of any of the species by soaking them in water to soften them. They are then pounded and rinsed repeatedly until the pulpy part is removed. The fibers may then be combed out, twisted into strands, and woven as desired.

Habitat and Distribution: In general, the Agave is found in dry ground throughout Arizona, New Mexico, southern Utah, southeastern California and into Mexico.

Description: Flowering stems, sometimes higher than a man's head, rise from a more or less woody base around which rise numerous spike-like succulent leaves. This plant is often confused with the yucca whose flowering stems are much shorter.

289. *Washingtonia filifera* (1) (Palm Family)
California Fan Palm

Preparation and Uses: The grape or berry-like

black fruits have a thin, sweet, edible pulp around an edible seed and may be eaten raw. The seed may be dried and ground into a fine-tasting meal.

Habitat and Distribution: The California Fan Palm is found in sandy or rocky washes in southeastern California, adjacent Arizona, and on into Mexico. It is a native plant that is becoming rare in nature, although extensively planted as an ornamental wherever it will grow in Arizona and California.

Description: This tree is a typical palm with a tall, columnar, gray trunk clothed in nature with a thatch of dead leaves. The large, green, heavy leaves have spiny margins and are roundish in shape and are borne in a cluster at the top. From the top area of the tree, fruit can be seen hanging in grapelike clusters.

290. *Ptelea pallida* and *angustifolia (baldwinii)*
     (2) (Rue Family)
     Hoptree, Baldwin's Hoptree

Preparation and Uses: The fruits of this plant have been used as a substitute for hops in brewing and may be ground, mixed with yeast, and used in bread to produce an exceptionally light loaf.

Habitat and Distribution: Hoptree is found in woods, canyons, and on slopes in southern Colorado and Utah, west to California and south to New Mexico, Arizona, and Mexico.

Description: These plants are shrubs to small trees with the leaves palmately divided into 3 leaflets. The flowers are borne in compound cymes.

291. *Dactyloctenium aegyptium* (1) (Grass Family)
     Crowfoot Grass

Preparation and Uses: The seeds may be dried and ground into flour for bread, or meal for cereal.

This plant, native to the Old World, was used by various peoples in Africa, and by a number of Arab groups.

Habitat and Distribution: The grass has become established in waste ground in California, Arizona, and New Mexico.

Description: Crowfoot Grass is a spreading annual with creeping stems bearing short, broad leaves. The stems end in 2 to several thick, finger-like, ascending to spreading spikes. The flower stem extends beyond the spikelets. The ripe seed is reddish brown and covered with a loose husk.

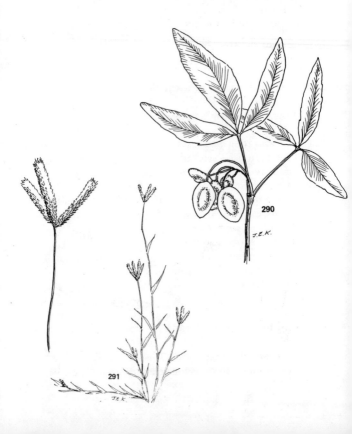

PLANTS OF THE ROCKY MOUNTAIN STATES

The few entries in this chapter in no way indicate the number of edible plants available in the Rockies. The reader should also consult the chapters on plants found throughout the West and the Northwest.

The Rocky Mountain area does not begin to have the diversity of climate that the Southwest and Northwest do. There does not seem to be much information on how the Indians of this area used edible plants, as their main food seems to have come through hunting. They had the plains with that enormous food supply, the buffalo herds. Then too, snow conditions made the Rockies inaccessible for the greater part of the year.

292. *Armeria leptophylla* (1) (Leadwort Family)
Thrift, Foxflower

Preparation and Uses: The bases of the plant may be washed, boiled with seasoning, and eaten.

Habitat and Distribution: The only record of this plant for the West comes from Colorado. It has been found at very high elevations (12,000 to 13,000 feet) in dry, rocky soil.

Description: This plant grows in dense tufts, and bears narrowly linear, sharp-pointed, soft leaves that are 1 to 4 inches long. The plant may or may not be hairy. The flower varies in color from pink to purple to whitish.

293. *Ipomoea leptophylla* (1) (Morning Glory Family)
Wild Potato Vine, Man-of-the-Earth,
Bush Morning Glory

Preparation and Uses: The flavor of the edible root of this plant apparently varies widely according to locality, growing conditions, and age. Some reports claim the root to be barely palatable, while others claim it to be delicious. This writer has not tried it.

As is often the case, the roots of young plants are best. They may be eaten raw, roasted, boiled, or dried for future use.

One should be careful to properly identify this plant as some species in this genus are purgative. *I. batatas* is the cultivated sweet potato.

Habitat and Distribution: Wild Potato Vine is found in dry, often sandy soil, mainly in plains areas, and not at high elevations, from Montana south into Texas and New Mexico.

Description: The plant is a perennial with deeply buried (and consequently hard to dig), huge roots, sometimes weighing 25 pounds or more. The plant is without hairs throughout, and has stems growing 1 to 4 feet long, mostly erect. The leaves are 2 to 6 inches long, linear to lanceolate, entire, and rather narrowly triangular or wedge-shaped, with short petioles. The flower stalks are short and bear 1 to 4 lavender to rose, funnel-shaped flowers.

294. *Lithospermun incisum* (1) (Borage Family)
Gromwell, Puccoon

Preparation and Uses: The roots may be eaten cooked.

Habitat and Distribution: Gromwell is found in dry soil on plains, foothills, and mountains in Montana, Wyoming, Colorado, Idaho, Utah, New Mexico, and Arizona.

Description: Gromwell is a many stemmed, rather hairy, perennial plant rising from a thick woody base and root. The somewhat hairy leaves are linear to narrowly oblong. The large flower is bright yellow.

295. *Geum rivale* (1) (Rose Family)
Purple Avens, Water Avens, Chocolate Root

Preparation and Uses: The root makes a chocolate-like drink when well boiled. Sugar is a good addition to the beverage.

In early times in England the root was often soaked for months in wine. Presumably a delicate flavor was imparted to the wine. This combination was supposed to be particularly good for the heart, preventing any troubles that might develop in that organ.

Habitat and Distribution: Purple Avens is found in meadows and boggy areas across Canada to British Columbia, south through the Western half of Colorado into New Mexico and on to the east. One would expect the plant to be found in Idaho and at least northern Washington but there is no good record of this.

Description: Purple Avens is an erect herb, 10 to 24 inches tall, with rather hairy, purplish stems. The pinnate, basal leaves are coarsely divided into obovate, doubly serrate leaflets. The purplish sepals are lanceolate to rather triangular in shape, and densely covered with long, soft hairs. The fan-shaped, purple-veined, clawed petals are flesh-colored, sometimes with a yellow tinge.

296. *Elaeagnus commutata* (1) (Oleaster Family) Silverberry

Preparation and Uses: The silver green berries may be eaten raw or cooked. They are good when used in soup and make an excellent jelly.

Habitat and Distribution: Silverberry is found along the banks of streams, or on hillsides, in Wyoming, Utah, Colorado, and Montana.

Description: This plant forms a shrub or small tree 6 to 15 feet in height, with twigs that are somewhat covered with brown, scale-like, or bran-like particles. The alternate leaves are silvery-scaly, and the berries are silvery-green.

297. *Ligusticum filicinum* (1) (Carrot Family) Loveroot, Lovage

Preparation and Uses: The green stems and roots are sweet and nutritious and may be eaten raw or cooked.

Habitat and Distribution: Loveroot is found in moist mountainous ground in northeastern Oregon, throughout Idaho, Montana, Wyoming, and the northern portions of Utah and Colorado.

Description: The plant is a smooth herbaceous perennial with a large aromatic root, large compound leaves with many leaflets divided in very narrow, linear segments. The flowers are white or pinkish.

298. *Viburnum pauciflorum* (1) (Honeysuckle Family)
Cranberry Tree, Mooseberry, High-Bush Cranberry

Preparation and Uses: The berries are edible raw and may be used in the same manner as the domestic cranberry, although the two plants are not related.

Habitat and Distribution: The Cranberry Tree is found in woods in Montana, Colorado, Wyoming, Idaho, Washington, and Oregon.

Description: This is a shrub 3 to 7 feet or more tall with broad, roundish leaves that narrow at the base, and have 3 terminal, toothed lobes, and 3 main veins. The undersurface of the leaves is hairy, the upper nearly smooth. The flowers are white, and the fruit is red.

299. *Liatris punctata* (1) (Sunflower Family)
Gayfeather, Blazing Star

Preparation and Uses: The root may be cooked and eaten.

Habitat and Distribution: This plant is found mostly east of the Continental Divide in dry, open often sandy areas in Montana, Wyoming, Colorado, New Mexico, and Mexico.

Description: Gayfeather is a perennial herb, 6 to 32 inches tall, rising from a branched, elongated rootstock. The linear, rather rigid, numerous, evenly distributed, punctate leaves are often hairy and thickened on the margins. The purple, rose or rarely white, rather crowded flower heads are in spikes.

300. *Ratibida columnifera* (1) (Sunflower Family)
Coneflower, Prairie Coneflower

Preparation and Uses: The leaves and flowers may be brewed into a pleasant tea.

Habitat and Distribution: Coneflower is a perennial herb with leafy stems rising from a more or less woody base. The alternate leaves are deeply pinnately divided into 5 to 13 linear to oblong divisions. The outside petals (ray flowers) of the flower are yellow to bluish or rose-purple. The center of the flower (disk flowers) is yellow.

301. *Tradescantia pinetorum* and *occidentalis*
(2) (Spiderwort Family)
Spiderwort

Preparation and Uses: Both plants may be eaten as greens. The roots of *T. pinetorum* are edible roasted or boiled.

Habitat and Distribution: *T. occidentalis* is found in sandy soil in Montana, Colorado, Wyoming, New Mexico, and Arizona, *T. pinetorum* is found in Arizona and New Mexico.

Description: Spiderworts are perennial and have thickened roots and a leafy stem above the ground. The leaves are narrow. The purple flowers are in a broad, flattened umbel, subtended by two or sometimes three bracts. The stamens number 6.

302. *Smilax herbacea* (1) (Lily Family)
Carrion Flower, Jacob's Ladder

Preparation and Uses: The young shoots, tendrils and all, may be cooked like asparagus. The tuberous roots may be used in the same way as those of the Greenbrier.

Habitat and Distribution: Carrion Flower is found in moist ground in woods and on edges of clearings in Montana, Wyoming, and Colorado.

Description: The plant is a vining or climbing herb with hairless stems and numerous oval to heart-shaped leaves. The curling tendrils on the stem at the base of each leaf stalk are quite distinctive. The greenish flowers are usually carrion scented, but are sometimes sweet-scented.

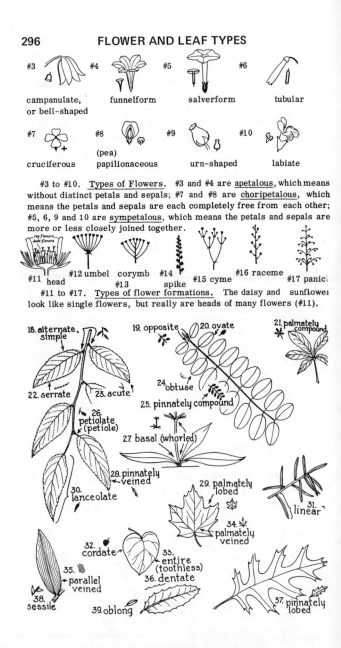

#3 campanulate, or bell-shaped

#4 funnelform

#5 salverform

#6 tubular

#7 cruciferous

#8 (pea) papilionaceous

#9 urn-shaped

#10 labiate

#3 to #10. <u>Types of Flowers</u>. #3 and #4 are <u>apetalous</u>, which means without distinct petals and sepals; #7 and #8 are <u>choripetalous</u>, which means the petals and sepals are each completely free from each other; #5, 6, 9 and 10 are <u>sympetalous</u>, which means the petals and sepals are more or less closely joined together.

#11 head   ray flowers   disk flowers

#12 umbel

#13 corymb

#14 spike

#15 cyme

#16 raceme

#17 panicle

#11 to #17. <u>Types of flower formations.</u> The daisy and sunflower look like single flowers, but really are heads of many flowers (#11).

18. alternate, simple

19. opposite

20. ovate

21. palmately compound

22. serrate

23. acute

24. obtuse

25. pinnately compound

26. petiolate (petiole)

27. basal (whorled)

28. pinnately veined

29. palmately lobed

30. lanceolate

31. linear

32. cordate

33. entire (toothless)

34. palmately veined

35. parallel veined

36. dentate

37. pinnately lobed

38. sessile

39. oblong

GLOSSARY

Alternate: Usually said of leaves when not opposite or whorled, but situated singly along the stem. Also said of other plant parts, such as stamens alternate (between) with the petals.

Anther: The enlarged, pollen-bearing part of the stamen.

Apex: The free end or tip of a plant part.

Axil: The upper angle between a branch or leaf with the stem.

Basal: Situated at or very near the base.

Bipinnate: Twice pinnate such as leaves that are pinnately compound with the leaflets again pinnately compound.

Blade: The expanded, usually flat, part of a leaf or flower petal.

Boil: Boiling a plant nearly always makes it easier to digest. Also, flavor can often be improved upon and the cook should not hesitate to add seasoning or other edibles to the pot.

Bract: A reduced or modified leaf subtending a flower.

Calyx: The outer, usually green, whorl of a flower as contrasted to the inner, usually showy whorl of the corolla or petals.

Cathartic: Purgative; generally used to mean that a cathartic will evacuate the intestine, sometimes so quickly as to cause diarrhea.

Catkin: A spike in which the flowers are usually of one sex and are nearly sessile.

Caudex: The woody base of a perennial herbaceous plant.

Cleft: Cut about halfway to the midrib.

Compound: Said when there are two or more similar parts in one organ as in a compound leaf with its leaflets.

Corolla: The inner part of a flower, usually showy, composed of the petals.

Cyme: A rather flattopped flower cluster wherein the central flowers bloom first; a flower cluster wherein the ones at the end of the stalk bloom before those below.

Deciduous: A cyclical falling off of plant parts such as flowers, fruits, leaves, etc., after a definite period of growth or function. Our most common application of this word is to leaves falling in autumn, but many desert plants lose their leaves in summer due to lack of water.

Disk flower: Flower heads in the Compositae, such as the sunflower, usually have two different kinds of flowers composing the overall blossom - tubular disk flowers on the large central disk and a ring of flattened, petal-like, ray flowers, usually of a different color, surrounding the central area of disk flowers.

Dissected: Divided into numerous segments - usually refers to leaves.

Diuretic: A diuretic increases water loss from body tissues and thereby increases the secretion and discharge of urine.

Divided: Divided to the base, usually referring to leaves that are parted to the midrib, or rachis.

Elliptic: Having a shape two or three times as long as wide. Refers mainly to leaf shape.

Entire: An undivided, continuous margin without teeth or indentations.

Ergot: A fungus infecting the fruiting bodies of numerous grasses. Ergot preparations have been used medicinally for several hundred years in uterine bleeding and childbirth. More recently ergot preparations have been used to treat migraine headaches. Many human and animal deaths have been recorded from eating ergot infected grain. The fungus is readily seen as a purplish or black growth, several times as long as the seeds of wheat, rye, oats, or other grass grains, coming from the seed-bearing tip. Although the fungal growth is easily seen, it breaks up so readily as to be rather unnoticeable when harvesting the grain. Fortunately, thorough washing of the grain will remove the fungus.

Fire pit: Dig a hole two feet wide and two to three feet deep or larger, line with thick flat rocks and build a fairly large fire in the hole to heat the rocks and provide hot ashes. After an hour to two hours of a hot fire, shovel out the ashes and coals. Place a thick layer of some wet green plant, such as grass, on the stones, place in food, usually wrapped in wet burlap, cover this with more grass, shovel on some moist soil or sand, and top with hot embers and a small fire. Keep the fire going until the food is done. Make a small hole with a stick to allow the entry of additional water. Most food will be done in 1 to 2 hours of steaming, but some, like a large roast, may require many hours.

Genus: The next larger unit of classification after species, species denoting only one particular kind of organism. The genus includes from one to many species.

Gland: Usually a small structure on a leaf, a stem, at the tip of a hair, etc., which usually secretes a sticky, often aromatic fluid. The structure may be a protuberance, an appendage, a depression, or entirely embedded within tissue.

Glume: The two lower empty bracts at the base of a grass spikelet.

Greens: In this book the word greens refers to those plants that may be cooked after the manner of any cultivated green vegetable, such as spinach.

Head: A dense cluster of sessile flowers arising from the summit, or very near the summit, of the flower stalk.

Herb: A plant that is not woody, at least above ground.

Imperfect: Lacking either functional stamens or pistils.

Infusion: To make an infusion of a plant material steep it in hot water without actually boiling.

Inserted: Attached to, borne upon, growing upon.

Irregular: Asymmetrical, not of regular shape or equal-sided.

Lanceolate: Lance-shaped, usually refers to leaves that are much longer than wide, and that taper to the apex from below the middle, and from there more abruptly back to the base.

Lateral: On the sides.

Leaflet: The leaf-like divisions of a compound leaf.

Linear: Long and narrow, such as a grass blade.

Lobe: A part of any plant organ set off by indentations.

Margin: Pertaining to the edge of a leaf or other organ.

Meal: Meal is generally considered to be more coarsely ground than flour, but can usually be used in the same way as flour. Indians in the West laboriously prepared meal and flour by grinding grain on a flat stone (metate) with another stone (mano) held in the hand. A few Indian groups in the West and many in Mexico still do this. Today one can quite effectively use a blender to grind meal, and the author knows of one person who uses a hand coffee grinder.

Membranaceous: Membrane-like; thin, pliable, soft.

Mush: Mush is usually made from meal and water, the amount of water depending on how thick a mush is desired. Mush is also prepared by mashing various plant parts in water.

Node: A more or less distinct joint of a stem where branches or leaves attach.

Nutlet: Nut-like, but small; used to describe any small, thick-walled, dry seed.

Ob: A latin prefix indicating the reverse condition.

Oblanceolate: The reverse of lanceolate in that the broadest portion of the leaf is above the middle and the sharpest point is at the base.

Obovate: Inversely ovate.

Opposite: Usually refers to two leaves at one node that appear opposite each other. Also refers to such items as a stamen opposite or in front of a petal.

Ovary: The basal part of the pistil containing the seeds.

Ovate: Flat and egg shaped with the broadest part near the base or below the middle.

Palmate: The veins or lobes radiating out from a common point.

Panicle: A compound flower cluster in which the main stem branches into secondary stems, these bearing the flower stems and flowers, or even branching indefinitely.

Pappus: The hair-like, feather-like, bristle-like, or scale-like projections at the tip of the fruit in most Compositae.

Parched: Toasted; cooked quickly in a dry pan or open flame until browned.

Pedicel: The stalk of a single flower.

Peduncle: The stalk of a flower or flower cluster.

Pemmican: Mix shredded, dried meat and dried berries with an equal amount of beef fat (obtained by frying chunks of raw beef fat trimmed from meat - usually obtainable in quantity from a meat market; do not use lard or commercial shortening). Pack this mixture in waterproof canvas or leather bags. Seeds or meal may be included. The amount of fat may be reduced to suit your taste. Pemmican will last for many months without spoiling. Indians used buffalo meat and fat, along with whatever berries were available.

Perfect: Having both functional pistil and stamens.

Perianth: The calyx and corolla together, especially when the two are similar.

Petals: One of the inner segments of a flower, usually colored.

Petiole: The stalk of a leaf.

Pinnate: A condition wherein the secondary veins of a leaf are arranged along the midrib, or when the leaflets of a compound leaf are arranged along a stalk and on each side of it.

Pinole: This Spanish word is usually used to refer to meal made from the seeds of wild plants, the meal often being a mixture of seeds.

Pistil: The ovary-containing, central organ of a flower.

Pith: The soft, spongy, usually white tissue found in the center of a stem, leaf stalk, or root.

Potherb: A potherb is any plant that is boiled to be eaten. Most should not be boiled long or with much water. Some have tough or fibrous tissues which require long boiling, however. Some must have the water changed one or more times to remove an undesirable flavor or compound. These plants are noted in the text.

Prostrate: Lying flat on the ground.

Punctate: Finely dotted with colored spots, punctures, or glands.

Purgative: Generally used to refer to something that will evacuate the intestine.

Raceme: An open, unbranched, elongate flower cluster arranged along an axis.

Radiate: Spreading outward from a common center.

Ray flower: Petal-like flowers surrounding the central disk in the Compositae. (see disk flower)

Receptacle: The base of the flower on which are borne the flower parts.

Regular: Used in describing a flower with radial symmetry, with each set of parts (petals, sepals, stamens, etc.) alike or symmetrical with each other.

Rhizome: An underground stem, often mistaken for actual roots, and frequently called rootstocks.

Roast: To bake in hot air, not in a flame, without water or cover. This may be done most easily in the open by placing the article to be roasted in the ashes of a campfire. Roasting can also be done by means of a spit or by placing the food in an oven.

Rosette: A cluster of crowded, basal, radiating leaves or other plant parts.

Salad plant: Any green plant that may be eaten raw. These plants can also be cooked.

Saponin: A chemical naturally found in many plants. Such plants often produce a good lather when crushed and rubbed in water. Saponin can often be boiled out of a plant, making that plant more edible. Too much saponin ingested can cause diarrhea. Commercial saponin has been used as a foaming agent in beverages and fire extinguishers.

Saprophyte: Usually used to refer to a plant that lives on dead organic matter.

Scurfy: Covered with small bran-like granules or scales.

Segment: A division or part of any organ.

Selenium: A nonmetallic, toxic element present in many western soils, and absorbed by some plants; causes livestock much trouble, and no doubt could cause human illness if eaten in sufficient quantity.

Sepal: One of the outermost flower-parts, usually green and usually just outside the petals.

Serrate: Having sharp-pointed teeth all pointing outward; sawtoothed.

Sessile: Without a stalk; attached directly by the base.

Sheath: The basal part of a leaf enclosing the stem.

Simple: Not compound.

Solitary: Alone, single.

Species: The basic unit of animal or plant classification, indicating an individual organism, as man, house, cat, dandelion, etc.

Spike: A raceme-like flower cluster, but with the flowers sessile.

Spikelet: A small spike, often used to refer to the flower-cluster of grasses.

Stamen: The pollen-bearing organ of a flower.

Steamed: To cook food in steam. Wild food is somehow always best when steamed in a fire pit, rather than in some other way.

Steep: To extract flavor or medicinal qualities from material by soaking it in hot, but not boiling, water.

Stigma: The apex of the pistil.

Stipule: Appendages, usually foliaceous or leaf-like, at the base of the petiole of some leaves.

Style: The narrow part of a pistil between the stigma and the ovary.

Terminal: At the end, summit, or apex.

Trifoliate: Having three leaflets.

Tufted: Closely or tightly clustered.

Umbel: A flattopped flower cluster whose individual flower stalks arise from the same place.

Unisexual: Flowers with only stamens or only pistils.

Vein: A strand of conducting and supporting tissue in a leaf or other organ.

Vestigial: The remnant or trace of a part of an organ that was once more fully developed.

Whorled: A ring of two or more similar organs, such as leaves, radiating from a node.

For absolute identification of a plant, or for more explicit regional information, the following books are helpful.

1. **Abrams, Leroy,** *Illustrated Flora of the Pacific States,* 4 vols., Stanford Univ. Press, Stanford, Calif., 1960. (This lifetime work of Leroy Abrams illustrates every species listed - expensive but well worth the cost.)

2. **Arnberger, Leslie P.,** *Flowers of the Southwest Mountains,* Southwestern Nat. Mon. Assoc., Globe, Arizona, 1953. (Inexpensive, illustrated paperback, good for identification.)

3. **Balls, Edward K.,** *Early Uses of California Plants,* Univ. of Calif. Press, Berkeley, 1962. (Small paperback listing a number of plants, not all of which are edible - thorough, interesting plant write-ups.)

4. **Craighead, John J.** and **Frank C.,** and **Ray J. Davis,** *A Field Guide to Rocky Mountain Wildflowers,* Houghton Mifflin Co., Boston, 1963. (Well illustrated - lots of color - typical of the good work done in the Peterson Field Guide series - good for identification - works well as far west as the east slope of the Cascade - Sierra Nevada mountain ranges.)

5. **Davis, Ray J.,** *Flora of Idaho,* Wm. C. Brown Co., Dubuque, 1952. (For the botanist or experienced amateur - no illustrations.)

6. **Dodge, Natt N.,** *Flowers of the Southwest Deserts,* Southwestern Monuments Assoc., Globe, Arizona, 1961. (Inexpensive, illustrated paperback, good for identification.)

7. **Fernald, Merritt L.,** and **A. C. Kinsey,** revised by **Reed C. Rollins,** *Edible Wild Plants of Eastern North America,* Harper and Row, N. Y., 1958. (An interesting book - a number of the plants listed are found in the West.)

8. **Harrington, H. D.,** *Manual of the Plants of Colorado,* Sage Books, Denver, 1954. (For the botanist or experienced amateur, a flora of Colorado, useful in all surrounding states - no illustrations.)

9. **Harrington, H.D.,** *Edible Native Plants of the Rocky Mountains,* Univ. of New Mexico Press, Albuquerque, 1967. (Interesting to read, with many good illustrations.)

10. **Jaeger, Edmund C.,** *Desert Wild Flowers,* Stanford Univ. Press, Stanford, Calif., 5th printing, 1950. (Includes many plants, many illustrations - good for identification in our southwestern deserts.)

11. **Kearney, Thomas H.,** and **Robert H. Peebles,** *Arizona Flora,* Univ. of Calif. Press, Berkeley, 1960. (For the botanist or experienced amateur - no illustrations.)

12. **Kingsbury, John M.,** *Poisonous Plants of the United States and Canada,* Prentice-Hall, Inc., Englewood Cliffs, N. J., 1964.

13. **McDougall, W. B.,** and **Herma A. Baggley,** *Plants of Yellowstone National Park,* Yellowstone Library and Museum Assoc., Yellowstone Park, Wyoming, 1956. (Well illustrated and useful for identification.)

14. **Medsger, Oliver P.,** *Edible Wild Plants,* MacMillan, N. Y., 1939. (Covers the United States and is an interesting book but not at all complete for the West.)

15. **Munz, Philip A.,** *California Desert Wildflowers,* Univ. of Calif. Press, Berkeley, 1962.

16. . . . ., *California Mountain Wildflowers,* Univ. of Calif. Press, Berkeley, 1963.

17. . . . ., *California Spring Wildflowers,* Univ. of Calif. Press, Berkeley, 1965.

18. . . . ., *Shore Wildflowers of California, Oregon, and Washington,* Univ. of Calif. Press, Berkeley, 1965. (These four books (15 - 18) are well illustrated and easy to use - good for identification.)

19. **Munz, Philip A.,** and **David D. Keck,** *A California Flora,* Univ. of Calif. Press, Berkeley, 1959. (Extremely thorough, extremely well-done, but for the botanist or experienced amateur - a few illustrations are included.)

20. **Patraw, Pauline M.,** *Flowers of the Southwest Mesas,* Southwestern Nat. Mon. Assoc., Globe, Arizona, 1953. (Inexpensive, illustrated paperback, good for identification.)

21. **Peck, Morton E.,** *A Manual of the Higher Plants of Oregon,* Binfords and Mort, Portland, 1961. (For the botanist or experienced amateur - no illustrations.)

22. **Saunders, Charles F.,** *Useful Wild Plants of the United States and Canada,* Robert McBride Co., N. Y., 1934. (Very limited for the West, but is enjoyable reading.)

23. **Sweet, Muriel,** *Common Edible and Useful Plants of the West,* Naturegraph Co., Healdsburg, Calif., 1962. (A small paperback which includes, as the title implies, useful plants other than edible ones - illustrated.)

24. **Weber, William A.,** *Rocky Mountain Flora,* Univ. of Colo. Press, Boulder, 1967. (More thorough than most would want but fairly easy to use and with quite a number of illustrations.)

INDEX OF PLANT USES
OTHER THAN FOOD

Scientific Names only listed

Fish Poisons:
Aesculus californica, 268
Chlorogalum pomeridianum, 276

Implements:
Cowania mexicana, 246
Olneya tesota, 258
Umbellularia californica, 220

Meat Tenderizer:
Asclepias, 70

Medicinal Plants:
The medicinal plants are listed according to the disorder they presumably help cure. The general location of each plant is listed according to w for West, nw for Northwest, sw for Southwest and r for the Rocky Mountain States.

Astringents:
Arctostaphylos uva-ursi, 66, w
Ephedra, 21, w

Cathartic:
Cornus, 125, 209, w
Croton tiglium, 221, sw
Frasera carolinensis, 70, w

Colds and Fevers:
Artemisia tridentata, 141, w
Cornus, 125, 209, w
Marrubium vulgare, 78, w
Pellaea mucronata, 218, sw
Rumex, 53, w

Diarrhea:
Cercis occidentalis, 253, sw
Vitis, 263, sw

NUTSHELL INDEX OF PLANT FOOD USES

Plant Numbers Only Listed

Bark:

85, 98, 182, 209, 266.

Berries:

Boiled:

62, 80, 82, 86, 89, 90, 107, 118, 120, 121, 154, 155, 194, 195, 196, 200, 209, 235, 241, 242, 252, 267, 269, 296, 298.

Dried and/or Ground:

53, 90, 241, 289.

Dried and/or Stored:

54, 62, 89, 90, 91, 107, 122, 195, 242.

Raw:

4, 7, 53, 54, 62, 80, 82, 86, 89, 90, 91, 107, 108, 118, 121, 122, 155, 156, 194, 195, 196, 200, 209 241, 242, 252, 267, 269, 273, 289, 296, 289.

Steamed:

195, 252.

Stewed:

53

Beverages:

Beers:

196, 244, 290

Juices:

44, 53, 56, 71, 75, 107, 108, 196, 214, 252, 256a, 268, 273, 285, 286, 287, 295, 302.

Teas:

3, 68, 72, 76, 77, 82, 84, 85, 93, 103, 105, 119, 140, 189, 197, 202, 206, 217, 221, 237, 249, 270, 300.

Breads & Cakes:

4, 6, 16, 32, 40, 41, 42, 45, 54, 90, 97, 101, 102, 116, 123, 125, 126, 165, 170, 174, 175, 176, 178, 181, 183, 185, 189, 191, 204, 213, 219, 252, 255, 256a, 256b, 258, 271, 285, 286, 288.

Bulbs:

Boiled:

34, 158, 159, 160, 161, 166, 167, 169, 281, 282.

Dried and/or Ground:

161.

Raw:

34, 159, 160, 161, 166, 169, 213.

Roasted:

34, 161, 167, 169, 281, 282.

Steamed:

161, 166, 213.

Candy:

37, 68, 87, 94, 137, 163, 173, 207, 210, 231, 256a, 274a.

Cereals:

182, 291.

Chewing Gum:

16, 129, 136, 142, 144, 145, 147, 188, 211.

Emergency:

37, 98, 170, 231, 266.

Flour & Meal:

4, 5, 6, 8, 9, 15, 16, 17, 20, 21, 23, 24, 25, 29, 32, 37, 40, 41, 42, 44, 45, 49, 51, 53, 67, 70, 75, 90, 92, 97, 98, 99, 101, 102, 112, 116, 123, 125, 126, 128, 153, 161, 165, 170, 172, 173, 174, 175, 176, 177, 178, 179, 180, 181, 182, 185, 186, 187, 191, 192, 204, 214, 215, 218, 219, 239, 241, 248, 250, 254, 255, 256a, 256b, 258, 261, 285, 286, 288, 289, 290, 291, 302.

Flowers & Buds:

Boiled and/or Brewed:
6, 19, 30, 37, 45, 59, 87, 105, 116, 127, 135, 148, 222, 246, 266, 275, 279, 283, 285, 290.

Dried and/or Brewed:
37, 93, 101, 127, 130,

Dried and/or Stored:
275.

Fried:
37, 263.

Raw:
37, 59, 65, 66, 87, 222, 246, 257, 266, 275, 279, 285.

Roasted:
66, 285.

Steamed:
37, 283.

Fruits:

Boiled:
37, 52, 199, 229, 230, 236, 238.

Dried and/or Ground:
37, 134, 229, 230, 250, 285.

Dried and/or Stored:
284.

Raw:
37, 52, 87, 99, 106, 134, 199, 201, 228, 229,230, 236, 251, 268, 284, 285.

Stewed:
37, 87, 88.

Grains:
175, 176, 181, 216.

Greens:

Boiled:

2, 6, 10, 11, 12, 19, 20, 21, 23, 24, 25, 26, 27, 28, 30, 31, 32, 35, 36, 37, 38, 39, 40, 41, 43, 44, 45, 47, 49, 51, 52, 57, 58, 60, 61, 64, 73, 76, 78, 93, 100, 101, 103, 111, 113, 116, 117, 125, 130, 131, 132, 135, 137, 138, 139, 140, 144, 145, 146, 148, 149, 154, 157, 158, 162, 165, 173, 181, 192, 193, 198, 208, 210, 214, 215, 220, 223, 224, 225, 227, 233, 234, 235, 245, 247, 256a, 276, 277, 278, 280, 283, 284, 286, 288, 292, 297, 301, 302.

Dried and/or Stored:

39, 76, 206, 234, 247, 280.

Raw:

2, 13, 16, 22, 27, 35, 52, 56, 57, 60, 93 111, 113, 117, 125, 137, 140, 145, 146, 148, 149, 157, 158, 165, 181, 192, 198, 203, 214, 223, 225, 233, 234, 247, 256a, 278, 280, 281, 283, 286, 288, 297, 301.

Roasted:

2, 38, 66, 193, 287.

Steamed:

2, 281, 283.

Jams & Jellies:

7, 37, 53, 54, 62, 77, 80, 82, 86, 87, 88, 89, 90, 91, 107, 120, 201, 214, 229, 230, 235, 267, 268, 296, 298, 302.

Juices:

44, 53, 56, 71, 75, 107, 108, 196, 214, 252, 256a, 268, 273, 285, 286, 287, 295, 302.

Mush:

4, 24, 32, 40, 41, 42, 53, 112, 143, 170, 178, 183, 187, 191, 239, 250, 252, 255, 256a, 256b, 275.

Raw:
22, 40, 45, 49, 55, 59, 69, 75, 93, 116, 123, 126,
128, 134, 170, 177, 178, 179, 180, 183, 184, 185,
192, 203, 279, 285, 286.

Roasted:
9, 15, 55, 66, 96, 125, 126, 128, 184, 202, 262,
279.

Roasted, Ground & Brewed:
119, 153.

Seasoning:
37, 112.

Soups & Broths:
9, 22, 37, 59, 90, 97, 103. 110, 111, 115, 123,
133, 155, 166 172, 185, 203, 214, 241, 296, 302.

Spreads:
25, 229.

Stews:
9, 22, 34, 37, 87, 90, 110, 111, 115, 143, 148, 152
155, 166, 172, 198, 214, 239, 241, 269, 302.

Syrup:
37, 59, 170, 229, 230, 256b, 272.

Teas:
3, 5, 68, 72, 76, 77, 82, 84, 85, 93, 103, 105, 116,
119, 127, 129, 130, 134, 140, 148, 153, 189, 197,
202, 206, 217, 221, 237, 249, 270, 300.

Water Supply:
37, 170, 231.

Wines:
53, 89, 90, 120, 148, 196, 229, 230, 268.

NOTES

NOTES

NOTES

NOTES

NOTES

NOTES

NOTES

NOTES